UNDERSTANDING GENERATIVE AI FOR BUSINESS LEADERS
DEMYSTIFYING STRATEGIC ADVANTAGE, ETHICAL DEPLOYMENT, AND PRACTICAL INTEGRATION FOR SUCCESS

SYNERGY AI EDITIONS

© **Copyright Synergy AI Editions 2024 - All rights reserved.**

The content within this book may not be reproduced, duplicated or transmitted without direct written permission from the author or the publisher.

Under no circumstances will any blame or legal responsibility be held against the publisher, or author, for any damages, reparation, or monetary loss due to the information contained within this book. Either directly or indirectly. You are responsible for your own choices, actions, and results.

Legal Notice:

This book is copyright protected. This book is only for personal use. You cannot amend, distribute, sell, use, quote or paraphrase any part, of the content within this book, without the consent of the author or publisher.

Disclaimer Notice:

Please note the information contained within this document is for educational and entertainment purposes only. All effort has been expended to present accurate, up-to-date, and reliable, complete information. No warranties of any kind are declared or implied. Readers acknowledge that the author is not engaging in the rendering of legal, financial, medical or professional advice. The content within this book has been derived from various sources. Please consult a licensed professional before attempting any techniques outlined in this book.

By reading this document, the reader agrees that under no circumstances is the author responsible for any losses, direct or indirect, which are incurred as a result of the use of the information contained within this document, including, but not limited to, — errors, omissions, or inaccuracies.

TABLE OF CONTENTS

Introduction   7

1. UNDERSTANDING AI: FROM BASICS TO BUSINESS TRANSFORMATION   9
   AI's Definition and Scope   9
   Why AI Matters: The Competitive Edge in Modern Business   13
   Generative AI Explained: Revolutionizing Creation and Innovation   15
   Decoding AI Jargon: A Glossary for Business Leaders   18
   The Evolution of AI: How We Got Here and Where We're Going   21

2. ALIGNING AI WITH STRATEGIC VISION AND VALUES   25
   Crafting Your AI Vision: Aligning with Business Objectives   26
   Building an AI-Ready Culture: Leadership and Mindset Shifts   28
   AI Investment Strategies: Where to Place Your Bets   31
   From Idea to Implementation: Developing Your AI Roadmap   34
   Measuring AI Success: KPIs and Metrics That Matter   37

3. INTEGRATING AI INTO THE CORE OF BUSINESS OPERATIONS   41
   Assessing Your AI Readiness: A Checklist for Businesses   42
   Overcoming Integration Challenges: Strategies and Solutions   44
   Ensuring Compatibility: AI and Legacy Systems   47
   Mitigating Disruption: Keeping Your Business Running Smoothly   50
   Case Study: Successful AI Integration in Retail   54

4. UNLOCKING THE AI-DRIVEN CUSTOMER
   EXPERIENCE   57
   Enhancing Customer Experiences with AI   57
   Streamlining Operations: AI in Supply Chain
   Management   60
   AI-Driven Decision Making: Transforming
   Leadership   63
   Innovating Products and Services through AI
   Insights   66
   Achieving Operational Excellence with Predictive
   Analytics   69

5. NAVIGATING THE ETHICAL TERRAIN OF AI   77
   Establishing an Ethical AI Framework   78
   Addressing Bias and Ensuring Fairness in AI
   Models   81
   Privacy and Data Protection: AI's Achilles' Heel   84
   Fostering Transparency and Accountability in AI
   Deployments   87
   Ethical AI Use Cases: Lessons from the Field   90

6. MITIGATING RISKS: SAFEGUARDING AI SYSTEMS   95
   Identifying Potential AI Security Risks   96
   Developing a Comprehensive AI Risk Management
   Plan   98
   Cybersecurity Measures for AI Systems   101
   Data Integrity and Protection in AI Operations   104
   Building Resilience: Preparing for AI-Related
   Contingencies   106

7. STAYING AHEAD: NAVIGATING THE AI
   REVOLUTION   111
   Tracking AI Trends: Resources and Tools for
   Leaders   112
   Innovating with AI: Fostering a Culture of
   Continuous Improvement   115
   AI and the Future of Work: Preparing Your
   Workforce   117
   Strategic Partnerships: Collaborating for AI Success   120
   The Next Frontier: Exploring Cutting-Edge AI
   Technologies   123

8. STEERING BUSINESSES THROUGH THE AI
   REVOLUTION   127
   Adopting a Visionary Mindset   127
   Building AI Literacy Across Your Organization   130
   Cultivating Ethical Leadership for AI Initiatives   133
   Leading by Example: AI Adoption Starts at the Top   137
   Empowering Teams for AI Innovation and Success   141

9. DEVELOPING AI TALENT WITHIN YOUR
   ORGANIZATION   145
   Conducting a Skills Audit   145
   Training and Upskilling: Creating an AI-Savvy
   Workforce   148
   Attracting Top AI Talent: Recruitment Strategies   151
   Cultivating a Collaborative Environment for AI
   Innovation   154
   Success Stories: Building World-Class AI Teams   157

10. LEVERAGING AI FOR TEAM DYNAMICS AND
    COLLABORATION   161
    AI Tools That Facilitate Team Collaboration   162
    Enhancing Creativity: AI's Role in the Creative
    Process   164
    Breaking Down Silos: AI as a Bridge Between
    Departments   167
    Fostering an Inclusive Culture Through AI
    Initiatives   170
    Case Study: AI-Driven Collaboration in
    Multinational Companies   173

    Conclusion   177
    References   181

INTRODUCTION

In an era where technology disrupts traditional business models, Artificial Intelligence (AI) emerges as both a monumental opportunity and a formidable challenge. Imagine a manufacturing floor where AI-enhanced robots and humans work in synergy, propelling productivity into realms once deemed fictional. This transformation is not a future speculation but a current reality across various industries, altering perceptions of work, innovation, and leadership. The imperative to adapt is pressing. As AI evolves rapidly, the divide between innovators and the hesitant expands. Statistics reveal that businesses adopting AI streamline operations and uncover new growth and customer engagement pathways. Ignoring AI can lead to obsolescence. This book aims to demystify AI for business leaders, providing a clear path to integrate AI into your operations, navigate ethical considerations, and leverage its potential for innovation and a competitive edge. Combining theoretical foundations with practical applications, we'll turn challenges into opportunities, ensuring your leadership excels in AI. Embark on a journey from understanding basic AI principles to mastering strategic integration, ethical deployment, and future-proofing your business against technological advancements. Alongside real-world examples, case studies, and actionable insights, this guide offers a pragmatic approach, focusing on industry-specific challenges and opportunities. We address common concerns like integration hurdles and the AI talent gap, aiming to boost confidence amid rapid change. Navigating the AI landscape becomes manageable and exhilarating with the proper knowledge and strategies. Embrace this journey with an open mind, ready to harness AI as a transformative force. Our goal is to keep up and lead, ensuring your business's prosperity in the digital age. Echoing Alan Kay's words, "The best way to predict the future is to invent it," let this book be your first step toward shaping a future where AI is a pivotal advantage. Welcome to "Understanding Generative AI for Business Leaders." Let's begin.

In business, a seismic shift occurs beneath our feet, its epicenter located squarely within the domain of Artificial Intelligence (AI). This evolution is not marked by the clamor of upheaval but by the quiet integration of AI into the fabric of daily operations, rendering businesses more efficient, innovative, and responsive to the needs of their customers. At the heart of this transformation lies not just the technology itself but a profound reimagining of what businesses can achieve when human ingenuity intersects with the capabilities of AI.

UNDERSTANDING AI: FROM BASICS TO BUSINESS TRANSFORMATION

AI'S DEFINITION AND SCOPE

Artificial Intelligence, in its broadest sense, refers to machines programmed to mimic cognitive functions such as learning, problem-solving, and decision-making—capabilities once thought exclusive to the human mind. The landscape of AI is vast, encompassing a range of technologies from simple automated responses to complex machine learning (ML) and deep learning models that process and interpret vast amounts of data in ways that mimic human neural networks. However, as AI becomes more advanced and integrated into various aspects of our lives, it also raises important ethical considerations. These include issues such as data privacy, algorithmic bias, and the potential for job displacement. It's important for businesses to be aware of these ethical considerations and to adopt AI in a responsible and ethical manner.

Machine learning, a subset of AI, involves the development of algorithms that enable machines to learn from and make predictions or decisions based on data. Deep learning, a further specialization within ML, utilizes layered neural networks to analyze patterns in data, facilitating advancements in image recognition, natural language processing, and even autonomous driving.

The Business Case for AI

The transition towards AI-driven operations is not merely a trend but a strategic imperative. Consider the efficiency gains from automating routine tasks, which allow employees to focus on higher-value activities that require human insight and creativity. Beyond mere efficiency, AI's predictive analytics can unearth insights from previously inaccessible data, offering businesses a deeper understanding of their operations, markets, and customers. This is not just about staying competitive, it's about leading the way in the AI revolution.

AI's transformative potential is not just a possibility but a reality that is reshaping industries. By synthesizing vast datasets, AI can identify trends and anomalies, supporting more informed strategic decisions. In customer service, AI-driven chatbots provide 24/7 assistance, improving customer experience while optimizing operational resources. These examples underscore AI's capacity not only to streamline operations but also to foster innovation, opening new avenues for products, services, and business models. This is the power of AI, and it's within your reach.

Transformation Stories

Real-world examples abound of businesses that have leveraged AI to remarkable effect. A notable instance is a global retailer that implemented machine learning algorithms to analyze customer behavior and preferences, resulting in highly personalized shopping experiences. This not only boosted customer satisfaction but also significantly increased sales. Another example is a healthcare provider that used AI to predict patient hospitalization risks based on electronic health records, improving patient outcomes while reducing unnecessary hospital admissions. In the financial sector, AI is used for fraud detection and risk assessment, while in manufacturing, it is used for predictive maintenance and quality control. These diverse applications highlight the versatility and potential of AI in various industries.

These stories highlight a dual truth: AI's vast potential, yet its most effective applications are profoundly contextual and tailored to each business's specific challenges and opportunities.

The Future Potential

The trajectory of AI's evolution points toward even greater integration into business and society. Emerging technologies such as generative AI, which can create new content—from writing to images—based on learned patterns, promise further to blur the lines between human and machine capabilities. As AI tools become more intuitive and aligned with natural human ways of working, their adoption will likely accelerate, embedding AI even more deeply into the workflow of businesses. Looking further ahead, AI could potentially revolutionize industries such as healthcare with personalized medicine, transportation with autonomous vehicles, and energy with smart grids. These future developments underscore the transformative potential of AI and the need for businesses to stay ahead of the curve in adopting and leveraging these technologies.

Yet, the future of AI in business is not solely about technological advancements. It is also about the expanding scope of possibility. AI has the potential to democratize expertise, making high-level analysis accessible to a broader range of businesses and functions. This means that businesses of all sizes and industries can potentially benefit from AI, not just those with large budgets or specialized technical expertise. It promises to redefine competitiveness, where the strategic use of AI can elevate a company's position in the market. Moreover, as AI technologies become more sophisticated and accessible, the opportunity for businesses to innovate—in products, services, and business models—expands exponentially.

The unfolding story of AI in business is one of transformation, innovation, and untapped potential. As leaders navigate this landscape, the imperative is clear: to understand AI not as a distant future or a disruptive force but as a present opportunity to redefine what is possible. However, it's crucial to approach AI adoption strategically, considering factors such as the business's unique needs and challenges, the readiness of the organization and its employees for AI integration, and the potential risks and benefits. A well-planned and strategic approach to AI adoption can ensure that businesses fully harness the potential of AI while mitigating any potential risks or challenges.

WHY AI MATTERS: THE COMPETITIVE EDGE IN MODERN BUSINESS

In an era where markets evolve at dizzying speed, the imperative for businesses to not only keep pace but set the pace becomes clear. This dynamic landscape, characterized by rapid technological advancements and shifting consumer expectations, necessitates tools and strategies that offer agility, foresight, and precision. Here, AI emerges as a technological innovation and a strategic asset, indispensable for maintaining a competitive edge in modern business.

The essence of competition has always hinged on the ability to anticipate and adapt to change faster than rivals. In this context, AI becomes a critical lever, enabling businesses to decipher emerging trends from big data noise, thereby staying ahead of the curve. It's the ability to process and analyze data at a scale and speed beyond human capacity that makes AI invaluable. For instance, once a time-consuming endeavor fraught with uncertainties, market analysis is transformed by AI into a swift, data-driven process that uncovers actionable insights, ensuring businesses can swiftly adapt to market shifts and consumer behaviors.

Moreover, the realm of decision-making, traditionally the bastion of human intuition and experience, is redefined by AI's capacity for data-driven analysis. Complex business decisions, from strategic investments to operational adjustments, benefit from AI's ability to offer a nuanced understanding of data patterns and trends. However, it's important to note that AI is not about replacing human decision-making but augmenting it with a level of depth and precision previously unattainable. The integration of AI into decision-making processes ensures that strategies are not just informed by data but are shaped by a comprehensive analysis that accounts for variables and correlations unseen to the naked eye. This means that human judgment and strategic thinking are still crucial in the decision-making process, with AI serving as a powerful tool to enhance these capabilities.

The personalization of customer experiences stands as another cornerstone of competitive advantage in the digital age. Personalization becomes the key to capturing attention and fostering loyalty in a market where consumers are bombarded with choices. AI, with its ability to analyze individual consumer behaviors and preferences, enables businesses to tailor experiences, recommendations, and communications at an individual level, at scale. This level of personalization, once the domain of boutique businesses with a limited clientele, is now accessible to companies of any size, allowing them to engage customers in a deeply personalized manner that drives satisfaction, loyalty, and, ultimately, business growth.

Operational efficiency, often the unsung hero of business success, is significantly enhanced by AI. By automating routine tasks and optimizing resource allocation, AI frees human talent to focus on areas where they add the most value—innovation, strategy, and customer engagement. Moreover, AI-driven predictive maintenance in manufacturing, for instance, anticipates equipment failures before they occur, minimizing downtime and associated costs. The operational agility afforded by AI reduces costs and improves the quality and speed of service delivery, factors directly linked to competitive advantage.

In the intricate dance of modern business, where the speed of digital transformation magnifies every step and misstep, AI emerges as a pivotal partner. It offers businesses the tools to navigate complexity with agility, make informed decisions, engage customers personally, and operate with unprecedented efficiency. This is not a future possibility but a current reality, where the strategic integration of AI into business operations is not just an option but a necessity for those looking to lead rather than follow.

GENERATIVE AI EXPLAINED: REVOLUTIONIZING CREATION AND INNOVATION

Generative AI emerges at the confluence of creativity and computation, redefining the innovation landscape across industries. Unlike traditional AI models designed to predict outcomes or classify data, generative AI ventures into the realm of creation, synthesizing new content, designs, and ideas that have never existed. It leverages complex algorithms to learn from vast datasets, not merely to mimic but to innovate, crafting outputs that reflect learned patterns yet exhibit novel characteristics.

At the heart of generative AI's distinctiveness is its ability to understand and replicate the nuances of human creativity. Whether it's composing music that resonates with human emotions, drafting articles indistinguishable from those written by seasoned journalists, or generating images that capture the subtleties of human artistry, generative AI transcends the traditional boundaries of machine capability. This leap from predictive analytics to creative synthesis marks a pivotal evolution in AI technology, heralding a new era where machines contribute to the analysis of the world and its enrichment.

The applications of generative AI span a broad spectrum, from practical to visionary. In product design, companies employ generative AI to conceive novel designs for everything from furniture to footwear, each iteration optimized for aesthetics, functionality, and sustainability. In marketing, brands leverage this technology to generate unique content, from advertising copy to personalized email campaigns, each piece tailored to resonate with its intended audience. The entertainment industry also finds generative AI a powerful ally, using it to script narratives, create virtual landscapes, and even compose musical scores, pushing the boundaries of creativity and offering audiences unprecedented experiences.

Beyond these applications, generative AI has profound potential for fostering business innovation. It acts as a catalyst for creative thinking, challenging teams to explore new possibilities and solutions. By generating many options and alternatives, generative AI expands the scope of conceivable, encouraging a departure from conventional thinking and exploring uncharted territories. This capacity to inspire and augment human creativity ensures businesses adapt to change and actively shape it, leading to innovation rather than following it.

Yet, the path to harnessing generative AI is full of challenges and ethical considerations. One of the primary concerns revolves around the issue of originality and copyright. As generative AI produces content that mirrors human creativity, discerning the line between inspiration and infringement becomes increasingly complex. This raises questions about the ownership of AI-generated content and the rights of those whose work trained the AI. Moreover, the potential for misuse of generative AI to create misleading or harmful content underscores the need for robust ethical frameworks and regulatory oversight. Ensuring that generative AI serves the greater good while respecting individual rights and creativity necessitates a concerted effort from developers, users, and policymakers alike.

Another challenge lies in integrating generative AI into existing workflows and processes. For businesses accustomed to traditional models of creation and innovation, adopting generative AI requires not just technological upgrades but a cultural shift. It necessitates an openness to new ways of working, where AI acts as a partner in the creative process, and outcomes are co-created by human and machine intelligence. This shift, while promising, demands flexibility, adaptability, and a commitment to continuous learning and development.

In addressing these challenges, businesses must also consider the implications of generative AI for the workforce. As AI takes on more creative tasks, the role of humans in the creative process evolves. Rather than rendering human creativity obsolete, generative AI amplifies it, freeing individuals from repetitive tasks and empowering them to focus on higher-level creative and strategic endeavors. This redefinition of roles underscores the importance of fostering skills that complement AI, such as critical thinking, empathy, and creativity, ensuring that the human workforce remains an indispensable pillar of innovation.

Generative AI, with its unparalleled capacity for innovation and creation, is a testament to the remarkable advances in AI technology. It offers a glimpse into a future where machines understand the world and contribute to its beauty and diversity. As businesses navigate the opportunities and challenges of generative AI, the potential for transformation is immense. From revolutionizing product design to reimagining content creation, generative AI promises to propel industries into new realms of creativity and innovation. Yet, realizing this potential requires careful consideration of the ethical and practical implications, ensuring that a commitment to responsible and inclusive innovation guides the journey toward this new horizon.

DECODING AI JARGON: A GLOSSARY FOR BUSINESS LEADERS

In the rapidly evolving landscape of artificial intelligence, the proliferation of technical jargon can often obscure the essence of discussions, rendering the subject matter impenetrable for those not steeped in the field's vocabulary. This section aims to demystify the lexicon of AI, offering clarity on terms that frequently populate conversations around technology and business strategy. Providing precise definitions and contextual applications fosters a deeper understanding of AI, moving beyond superficial engagement with buzzwords to grasp their underlying significance and implications for business.

Key Terms Explained

At the foundation of AI lies a suite of terms whose understanding is crucial for any business leader. **Machine Learning (ML)**, for instance, refers to algorithms that enable computers to learn from and make predictions on data, bypassing the need for explicit programming for each new piece of information. Similarly, **Deep Learning**, a subset of ML, involves:

- Neural networks with multiple layers.
- Allowing machines to process data in complex, human-like ways.
- Enhancing their ability to recognize patterns and make decisions.

Natural Language Processing (NLP) is another pillar. It enables machines to understand and interact using human language, transforming how businesses engage with customers through chatbots and virtual assistants. Meanwhile, **Predictive Analytics**

harnesses ML to analyze data and predict future events, offering businesses foresight into customer behavior, market trends, and operational risks.

Contextualizing AI Terms

The practical application of these terms reveals their relevance to business operations and strategy. For example, ML powers recommendation engines on e-commerce platforms, analyzing customer data to predict and suggest products, thereby personalizing the shopping experience and boosting sales. In manufacturing, predictive analytics enables preemptive equipment maintenance, analyzing operational data to forecast failures before they occur, reducing downtime and maintenance costs.

NLP finds application in enhancing customer service, powering chatbots that offer personalized, efficient interactions by understanding and processing user queries in natural language. Similarly, deep learning advances visual recognition systems, improving quality inspection processes in manufacturing by identifying defects with greater accuracy than human inspectors.

Beyond Buzzwords

Engaging with these terms requires an acknowledgment of their practical implications, encouraging a shift from passive consumption of jargon to active exploration of its significance. Understanding that ML can drive efficient decision-making, cost reduction, and revenue growth prompts leaders to consider how their businesses can adopt these technologies. Recognizing NLP's role in enhancing customer interaction leads to strategic investments in AI-driven communication tools, elevating the customer experience and operational efficiency.

This shift necessitates a critical approach to AI discussions, questioning how each term and technology aligns with and can advance business objectives. It involves scrutinizing the feasibility, scalability, and potential ROI of AI initiatives, ensuring that strategic considerations and a clear understanding of expected outcomes guide investments in technology.

Staying Informed

As AI evolves, staying abreast of new developments and terminology becomes imperative for business leaders. This entails regular engagement with industry publications, attending conferences, and participating in forums where AI innovations are discussed. It also fosters an organizational learning culture, encouraging teams to explore AI advancements and consider their applications in business contexts.

Subscribing to newsletters from leading AI research institutions and technology firms offers insights into cutting-edge developments and emerging terms. At the same time, online courses and workshops provide deeper dives into specific AI technologies and their business applications. Engaging with these resources enhances understanding and sparks ideas for leveraging AI to drive innovation and competitive advantage.

In this dynamic landscape, business leaders' roles extend beyond mere familiarity with AI terminology to active engagement with the technologies and concepts these terms represent. It involves a commitment to ongoing education, a willingness to question and explore AI's implications for business strategy, and an openness to integrating new technologies in pursuit of operational excellence and innovation.

By demystifying AI jargon and embracing the technologies it encompasses, leaders can navigate the complexities of the digital age, transforming challenges into opportunities for growth and innovation. This journey, marked by continuous learning and strategic adaptation, positions businesses to survive and thrive in an era of rapid technological advancement and change.

THE EVOLUTION OF AI: HOW WE GOT HERE AND WHERE WE'RE GOING

The narrative of artificial intelligence unfolds like a tapestry woven from threads of ambition, innovation, and relentless pursuit of understanding. This fabric, rich with the endeavors of scientists, engineers, and visionaries, traces back to the mid-20th century when the concept of a machine capable of mimicking human intelligence first took shape. The initial milestones in AI, marked by the development of simple algorithms and theoretical models, laid the groundwork for a field that would, in time, revolutionize the interaction between humans and machines.

In these formative years, AI's potential was glimpsed in laboratories and academic institutions where pioneering figures like Alan Turing questioned the limits of machine intelligence. Turing's eponymous test, proposed as a measure of a machine's ability to exhibit intelligent behavior indistinguishable from a human, encapsulated the era's aspirations. Throughout the subsequent decades, progress ebbed and flowed, with periods of vigorous activity giving way to so-called AI winters, times when expectations outpaced results, leading to reduced interest and funding. Yet, through cycles of optimism and disillusionment, the foundation was set, embedding AI's principles in the fabric of technological advancement.

The acceleration of AI innovation, particularly in the last two decades, owes much to a confluence of factors. Breakthroughs in computational power, alongside the exponential growth of data, have propelled AI from theoretical possibility to practical reality. The advent of the internet and the digitization of information have created a data-rich environment in which AI algorithms can learn and evolve. Moreover, advancements in neural networks, inspired by the structure and function of the human brain, have enabled machines to process and interpret complex data with unprecedented sophistication. These neural networks, layered in deep learning algorithms, now underpin some of the most advanced AI applications, from image and speech recognition to natural language processing.

The current state of AI, a reflection of this rapid evolution, is characterized by diversity and depth. AI technologies have permeated various sectors, transforming operations, products, and services. In healthcare, algorithms analyze medical images with a precision that rivals, and in some cases surpasses, human experts, facilitating early diagnosis and personalized treatment plans. AI enhances risk assessment, fraud detection, and customer service in finance, offering more secure and tailored experiences. Meanwhile, in consumer technology, AI-powered virtual assistants navigate users through their digital lives, responding to queries, organizing schedules, and even controlling smart home devices.

The proliferation of AI applications has also spurred discussions on ethics, governance, and the future of work. As AI systems take on more complex tasks, the need for guidelines that ensure their ethical use, transparency, and accountability becomes paramount. Simultaneously, integrating AI into workplaces prompts a reevaluation of skills and roles, highlighting the importance of adaptability and lifelong learning.

Looking forward, the trajectory of AI development points to a horizon brimming with potential and challenges. The emergence of generative AI, capable of creating original content, opens new avenues for creativity and innovation across industries. From generating novel drug compounds to designing custom products, this facet of AI promises to unlock a new level of problem-solving and invention.

Concurrently, the advancement of AI in understanding and generating human language hints at a future where machines can communicate more intuitively, breaking down barriers between human-machine interaction. This progress in natural language processing could revolutionize education, making knowledge more accessible and learning more personalized.

Yet, as AI systems become more autonomous and decision-making shifts from human to machine, the implications for society, ethics, and governance grow more complex. The potential for bias, privacy concerns, and the need for oversight will drive discourse on balancing innovation with responsibility. Ensuring that AI serves the greater good and enhances human capabilities without diminishing human dignity will require a collective effort from technologists, policymakers, and society.

Businesses stand at the crossroads of opportunity and obligation in this dynamic landscape. The ability to leverage AI for competitive advantage, driving efficiency, innovation, and growth, is matched by the responsibility to do so in an ethical, transparent, and inclusive manner. As AI continues to evolve, its integration into business strategy and operations will not just be about technological adoption but about navigating the complexities of a changing world.

The evolution of AI, from its theoretical origins to its current state and beyond, mirrors humanity's quest for knowledge and mastery over its environment. It reflects an ambition to extend the boundaries of what is possible, using technology to replicate human intelligence and complement and augment it. As we stand on the threshold of discoveries and applications, the journey of AI remains as much about charting the future as it is about understanding our place within it.

ALIGNING AI WITH STRATEGIC VISION AND VALUES

Leaders find themselves at a crucial inflection point in an era where business landscapes morph with the relentless pace of technological advancements. Artificial Intelligence (AI) stands at the forefront of this evolution, not merely as a tool for operational optimization but as a catalyst for profound organizational transformation. This chapter delves into the foundational aspect of integrating AI into business strategy: the crafting of an AI vision that not only resonates with the core objectives and values of the organization but also serves as a strategic guidepost, illuminating the path toward a future where AI is a key driver of business success.

CRAFTING YOUR AI VISION: ALIGNING WITH BUSINESS OBJECTIVES

Defining Your AI Goals

Setting the compass towards the future entails a vision and a roadmap marked by clearly defined objectives. When delineating AI initiative goals, aligning with overarching business objectives becomes paramount. This alignment ensures that AI serves as a lever, amplifying the strategic direction rather than diverting resources into siloed technological pursuits. For instance, if a primary business objective is to enhance customer satisfaction, an AI goal might focus on personalizing customer interactions through machine learning algorithms. This specificity ensures that AI initiatives directly impact strategic business outcomes, transforming abstract possibilities into tangible results.

The Role of Leadership

Leadership in the AI era transcends traditional paradigms, demanding a blend of visionary foresight and pragmatic execution. Leaders are not just the architects of the AI vision but also the driving force behind its realization. They are tasked with the dual responsibility of championing AI initiatives and ensuring their alignment with the organization's mission. This role involves not just endorsement but active participation in defining AI goals, understanding their potential impact, and communicating their value throughout the organization. The commitment of leadership to the AI vision serves as a beacon, guiding teams through the complexities of implementation and fostering an environment where AI can thrive.

Aligning AI with Core Values

In the integration of AI, the preservation of an organization's core values stands as a critical consideration. AI initiatives should not only reflect these values but also reinforce them, embedding them into the technological fabric of the organization. For a company that prioritizes sustainability, for example, AI could be leveraged to optimize resource use or reduce waste in manufacturing processes. This alignment ensures that AI initiatives resonate with the organization's ethos, fostering a sense of purpose and cohesion. It also serves as a reminder that technology, in its most impactful form, amplifies human values, driving progress that is both innovative and principled.

Long-Term Visioning

The horizon of AI extends far beyond immediate gains, beckoning leaders to envisage how AI can catalyze long-term transformation. This long-term vision involves contemplating AI's potential to redefine market positions, create new value propositions, and even alter business models. Consider the implications of generative AI in product design, opening avenues for customization and innovation previously constrained by human bandwidth. Leaders must navigate this terrain with an eye toward the future, balancing the allure of short-term wins with the transformative potential of sustained AI integration.

Interactive Element: Crafting Your AI Strategy Workbook

This section includes an interactive workbook to facilitate the translation of these concepts into actionable strategies. The workbook guides leaders through a series of reflective questions and exercises designed to:

- Clarify the organization's long-term objectives and how AI can support these goals.
- Identify core values and explore how AI initiatives can embody these principles.
- Envision the transformative potential of AI within the organization and industry.

This tool serves not only as a blueprint for developing an AI vision but as a living document that evolves with the organization's journey through AI integration.

By anchoring AI initiatives in the organization's strategic objectives and values, leaders can ensure that technology serves as a true partner in achieving business success. Crafting an AI vision, therefore, becomes an exercise in strategic alignment, leadership commitment, and value integration, setting the stage for AI to drive meaningful and sustainable transformation.

BUILDING AN AI-READY CULTURE: LEADERSHIP AND MINDSET SHIFTS

Fostering AI Literacy

In the labyrinth of technological advancement, the beacon that guides an organization toward an AI-ready culture is the widespread literacy of AI across all echelons. This literacy transcends the mere understanding of AI's mechanics to embrace its potential and pitfalls. Strategic initiatives might include targeted workshops tailored to different departmental needs, fostering an environment where curiosity about AI is nurtured and rewarded. Imagine a series of immersive sessions where marketing teams explore AI's power in consumer behavior prediction while the operations staff delves into logistics optimization through AI-driven analytics. Such initiatives democratize AI knowledge, ensuring it's not siloed within tech departments but permeates the entire organization, fostering a collective vision where every member grasps AI's role in their sphere of influence.

The Importance of a Growth Mindset

At the core of an AI-ready culture lies the cultivation of a growth mindset, a belief in the boundless potential of individuals and organizations to evolve through effort, strategy, and constructive feedback. This mindset is crucial in AI adoption, where the terrain is marked by rapid evolution and the occasional setback. It encourages an ethos where 'failures' are not dead-ends but stepping stones, rich with insights that pave the way for refinement and progress. For instance, an AI project that does not yield the anticipated efficiency gains on the first trial becomes a crucible for learning, prompting a reassessment of data inputs or algorithm suitability. In such an environment, experimentation is tolerated and celebrated as a vital component of innovation, ensuring that teams remain agile, resilient, and perpetually attuned to improvement opportunities.

Cross-Functional Collaboration

Integrating AI into business processes reconfigures traditional departmental boundaries, necessitating unprecedented cross-functional collaboration. This collaboration becomes the engine driving AI solutions that are both technologically sound and deeply aligned with business goals. Consider the synergy between data scientists and marketing professionals collaborating to refine customer segmentation algorithms, ensuring they encapsulate nuanced market dynamics. Or engineers working alongside HR to develop AI-driven talent recruitment and retention tools. Such collaboration fosters a holistic approach to AI implementation, where diverse perspectives converge to create innovative, practical, and strategically coherent solutions.

Change Management

Navigating the organizational metamorphosis accompanying AI adoption demands a sophisticated approach to change management. This process begins with clearly articulating the AI vision, translating abstract concepts into tangible impacts that resonate with stakeholders at all levels. Communication is key, employing a variety of channels to ensure the message not only reaches but engages the audience, fostering an understanding of AI's role in the organization's future. Moreover, change management encompasses the meticulous planning of the transition phase, ensuring resources are in place, timelines are realistic, and support systems are available to address concerns and challenges that arise. It also involves recognizing and celebrating milestones, reinforcing the value of the AI journey, and keeping the momentum alive. For example, sharing success stories of AI-driven improvements within the organization can galvanize support and enthusiasm, turning skeptics into advocates.

Leadership and mindset shifts play pivotal roles in this intricate dance of building an AI-ready culture. They transform the organizational landscape, preparing it to adopt AI and thrive with it. Organizations can navigate the complexities of AI integration through initiatives that enhance AI literacy, cultivate a growth mindset, foster cross-functional collaboration, and adeptly manage change. This journey reshapes not only how businesses operate but also how they envision their future in a world where

AI's potential is boundless, and the opportunities for innovation are limitless.

AI INVESTMENT STRATEGIES: WHERE TO PLACE YOUR BETS

In the dynamic theatre of business technology, where artificial intelligence (AI) plays a starring role, leaders face pivotal decisions on where to allocate resources to harness AI's transformative power. The essence of strategic AI investment lies not merely in the allure of cutting-edge technology but in the meticulous analysis and alignment with business imperatives. This section unfurls a tapestry of considerations for steering AI investments towards areas of maximal impact, ensuring a harmonious balance between innovation's promise and the pragmatism of risk and reward.

Assessing AI Opportunities: Framework for Identifying Where AI Can Create the Most Value in Your Business

Navigating the vast landscape of AI opportunities requires a discerning eye to distinguish between fleeting trends and genuine value drivers. A structured framework, anchored in a deep understanding of business operations, customer needs, and market dynamics, becomes indispensable. This approach begins with an exhaustive inventory of business processes, identifying bottlenecks, inefficiencies, and areas ripe for enhancement or innovation. Engaging in dialogue with cross-functional teams offers diverse perspectives, uncovering latent needs and opportunities that AI could address. Concurrently, a vigilant gaze on industry trends and competitive benchmarks reveals where AI is setting new performance or customer experience standards. Prioritization emerges from this confluence of insights, guided by strategic alignment, potential impact, feasibility, and scalability criteria. This rigorous process delineates a roadmap where AI investments are not scattergun but strategically targeted, promising substantive advancements in operational excellence, customer engagement, or market differentiation.

Balancing Risk and Reward: Discuss How to Approach Risk Management When Investing in AI Technologies

The allure of AI's potential must be tempered with a sober evaluation of associated risks, crafting a balanced portfolio of AI initiatives that span the spectrum from safe bets to high-reward ventures. Diverse methodologies, from predictive modeling to scenario analysis, illuminate risk contours, encompassing technical feasibility, data privacy concerns, ethical implications, and integration challenges. This illumination informs the development of mitigation strategies, such as phased rollouts, robust data governance frameworks, and ethical AI guidelines, ensuring risks are not merely identified but actively managed. Moreover, a dynamic approach to risk assessment, revisited regularly, adapts to evolving technologies, market conditions, and regulatory landscapes. Through this careful calibration of risk and reward, organizations navigate the tumultuous waters of AI investment with resilience, poised to seize opportunities while safeguarding against adverse outcomes.

Funding AI Initiatives: Explore Various Funding Options for AI Projects, Including Internal Budgeting and External Financing

Securing the lifeblood of AI initiatives—funding—demands a strategic approach, blending internal allocations with external financing avenues to fuel ambitious AI agendas. Internal budgeting, leveraging existing IT and innovation allocations, offers a direct route, requiring robust business cases to unlock funds. These cases articulate the strategic rationale, projected impacts, and financial metrics underpinned by compelling evidence from pilots or market analysis. For ventures beyond the reach of internal resources, external financing introduces a spectrum of options, from venture capital and corporate venture arms eager to invest in groundbreaking applications to government grants supporting AI innovation in strategic sectors. Strategic partnerships with technology providers or academic institutions also emerge as creative funding mechanisms, offering access to cutting-edge AI capabilities and research in exchange for shared risks and rewards. This multifaceted approach to funding ensures AI initiatives are not constrained by capital but propelled by a judicious blend of internal and external resources.

ROI Expectations: Set Realistic Expectations for the Return on Investment from AI Projects and How to Measure Success

Anchoring AI initiatives in financial realism ensures investments transcend technological fascination to deliver tangible business value. Setting ROI expectations begins with clearly articulating value drivers, whether cost reduction, revenue growth, customer satisfaction, or competitive advantage. Quantifying these impacts, though challenging, relies on a combination of historical data, industry benchmarks, and predictive analytics, yielding a spectrum of potential outcomes. Equally crucial is acknowledging the time horizon for ROI realization, recognizing that AI projects may entail upfront investments and learning curves before yielding dividends. This temporal dimension underscores the importance of interim metrics—operational efficiencies, customer engagement indices, or innovation rates—that signal progress toward long-term financial goals. Transparent communication of these expectations and metrics, tailored to stakeholder groups from the boardroom to the frontline, fosters a shared understanding of AI's value proposition. In this realm, success is not merely measured by financial returns but by strategic advancements, positioning AI as a pivotal axis around which future business growth and innovation revolve.

FROM IDEA TO IMPLEMENTATION: DEVELOPING YOUR AI ROADMAP

In the crucible of technological innovation, the path from the genesis of an AI idea to its full-scale execution unfolds with meticulous planning and adaptive execution. This odyssey demands a vision and a tangible, actionable roadmap that charts the course from conceptualization to realization. The intricacies involved in breathing life into AI initiatives necessitate a structured approach, where the blueprint encompasses the identification of strategic priorities, initiating pilot endeavors, expanding successful prototypes, and vigilant oversight of ongoing projects.

Planning Your AI Journey

An effective AI roadmap's genesis lies in distilling strategic priorities into executable projects. This necessitates a granular dissection of organizational goals, a rigorous evaluation of existing technological infrastructure, and a candid assessment of in-house versus outsourced AI competencies. Drawing from the wellspring of insights across business units, a multidisciplinary task force becomes instrumental in translating these priorities into specific AI initiatives. Armed with diverse perspectives, this collective undertakes the critical task of sequencing projects, not merely by their strategic importance but through an astute assessment of dependencies, resource requirements, and potential impacts. This planning phase, thus, becomes a dynamic process where flexibility intertwines with strategic intent, ensuring the roadmap is both ambitious and grounded in operational realities.

Pilot Projects and Prototyping

The initiation of pilot projects serves as the proving ground for AI initiatives, a space where hypotheses are tested and assumptions meet the rigor of real-world application. These preliminary ventures, characterized by their limited scope and scale, offer invaluable insights into AI solutions' feasibility, potential impact, and adjustment needs. For instance, a pilot project aimed at enhancing customer service through natural language processing tools may reveal unforeseen challenges in understanding regional dialects or slang, necessitating refinements in the AI model. The importance of these pilots transcends mere technical validation; they act as catalysts for organizational learning, fostering a culture of innovation and resilience. As such, the selection of pilot projects demands a strategic lens, prioritizing initiatives that promise to deliver quick wins and generate learnings that can ripple across the organization, informing broader AI strategy.

Scaling AI Solutions

The transition from successful pilot projects to organization-wide AI integration embodies the principle of scaling, a phase where proven AI solutions extend their reach, magnifying their impact. This scaling process, however, is not a mere expansion but a thoughtful adaptation, where solutions are customized to fit the diverse needs and contexts across the organization. It involves meticulously evaluating infrastructure readiness, data scalability, and the potential need for retraining AI models to accommodate varied datasets. Moreover, this phase is underscored by establishing governance frameworks that ensure AI solutions adhere to ethical standards, data privacy regulations, and operational best practices. Effective scaling thus demands a balance between technical precision and organizational adaptability, ensuring AI solutions expand in reach, relevance, and efficacy.

Monitoring and Iteration

Vigilant monitoring and continual iteration form the backbone of sustainable AI initiatives. This ongoing process transcends performance tracking to encompass a comprehensive evaluation of AI projects against predetermined metrics and objectives. Advanced analytics and visualization tools play a pivotal role, offering real-time insights into AI solutions' performance, adoption, and business impact. Yet, the essence of this phase lies in the readiness to iterate and refine AI models and strategies in response to emerging data, feedback, and changing business landscapes. Here, AI projects are imbued with resilience and empowered to evolve in alignment with organizational growth and technological advancements. This iterative process, underscored by a commitment to learning and adaptation, ensures AI initiatives remain agile, effective, and aligned with the organization's strategic imperatives.

In navigating the complexities of AI implementation, organizations are called upon to embark on a journey that is as strategic as it is adaptive. From the meticulous planning of AI roadmaps to the strategic initiation of pilot projects, the thoughtful scaling of successful endeavors, and the vigilant monitoring and iteration of ongoing initiatives, the path to AI integration is marked by continuous learning, strategic foresight, and operational agility. Through this structured yet flexible approach, AI initiatives transcend the realm of possibility to become tangible drivers of innovation, efficiency, and competitive advantage.

MEASURING AI SUCCESS: KPIS AND METRICS THAT MATTER

In the vast and intricate landscape of AI implementation, identifying and monitoring key performance indicators (KPIs) emerge as vital navigational tools. These metrics, carefully selected and rigorously tracked, illuminate the path of AI initiatives, offering clear signposts of progress and areas needing recalibration. This meticulous approach to measurement eschews one-size-fits-all solutions, advocating instead for a nuanced understanding of success that aligns with specific organizational goals and the unique attributes of each AI project.

Selecting the Right KPIs

The foundation of effective AI assessment lies in the strategic selection of KPIs that resonate with the objectives at hand. This selection process demands a discerning analysis, distinguishing between generic metrics and those that truly capture what an organization seeks to achieve with AI. For instance, if an AI project aims to enhance customer service efficiency, relevant KPIs include response times, resolution rates, and customer satisfaction scores. Conversely, an initiative focused on improving supply chain logistics could prioritize metrics such as inventory turnover rates, shipping times, and cost reductions per shipment. This targeted approach ensures that KPIs serve as accurate reflections of success, tailored to each AI endeavor's specific ambitions and operational realities.

Quantitative and Qualitative Measures

An expansive view of AI success encompasses quantitative metrics and qualitative feedback, weaving together a tapestry of insights that capture the multifaceted impact of AI. Quantitative measures, grounded in data, offer objective performance benchmarks, from increased sales and reduced costs to enhanced accuracy and speed in operations. Yet, the story of AI's influence extends beyond numbers into qualitative feedback that sheds light on the subtler dimensions of AI integration. Employee feedback on AI tools' usability, customer anecdotes about enhanced experiences, and partner testimonials on improved collaborations add depth to understanding AI's value. Combining hard metrics with soft feedback, this dual lens furnishes a holistic view of AI success, capturing its tangible and intangible benefits.

Benchmarking and Progress Tracking

Navigating the competitive terrain of AI implementation, organizations look to benchmarking as a compass, orienting their progress against industry standards and best practices. This comparative analysis offers a dual advantage, highlighting areas of competitive advantage and pinpointing opportunities for improvement. Tracking progress over time through regular reviews of KPIs and benchmarks enables organizations to chart their AI journey with precision. Adjustments and interventions become data-driven decisions calibrated to the evolving landscape of AI capabilities and market dynamics. This dynamic process of benchmarking and progress tracking fosters a culture of continuous improvement, where AI initiatives are not static investments but evolving assets that adapt to new challenges and opportunities.

Learning from Data

At the heart of AI's transformative power lies its ability to generate and analyze vast data, offering unprecedented insights into operations, customer behaviors, and market trends. Leveraging the data generated by AI systems becomes a strategic imperative, transforming raw information into a wellspring of knowledge that informs decision-making and drives continuous improvement. This entails not just the collection and storage of data but its active analysis to uncover patterns, trends, and anomalies that can inform strategic adjustments. For example, data on customer interactions with AI-powered service platforms can reveal preferences and pain points, guiding enhancements to the customer experience. Similarly, operational data from AI-driven logistics solutions can identify bottlenecks and inefficiencies, prompting process optimizations. In this way, learning from AI-generated data becomes a cyclical process, where insights fuel refinements, generating new data and perpetuating a cycle of learning and improvement.

In the intricate dance of AI integration, measuring success through KPIs and metrics emerges as a vital discipline, ensuring that AI initiatives remain aligned with organizational goals and responsive to the dynamic landscapes in which they operate. The strategic selection of KPIs, balanced assessment through quantitative and qualitative measures, rigorous benchmarking and progress tracking, and continuous learning from AI-generated data constitute the pillars of this discipline. Together, they furnish a comprehensive framework for assessing AI's impact, guiding organizations in pursuing innovation and competitive advantage.

As we transition from meticulously examining AI's strategic alignment and measurement to exploring its operational integration, the journey ahead promises insights into the practical challenges and opportunities of weaving AI into the fabric of business operations. This shift from strategy to execution underscores the symbiotic relationship between vision and action, where the aspirations of AI integration meet the realities of its implementation.

INTEGRATING AI INTO THE CORE OF BUSINESS OPERATIONS

In an era where the digital and the tangible intertwine more closely than ever, businesses stand at the threshold of a transformation led not by the mere adoption of new technologies but by their seamless integration into the very sinews of organizational operations. Artificial Intelligence (AI), with its myriad capabilities, offers a beacon for this transformation, promising enhancement and a redefinition of operational efficiency, customer engagement, and innovative prowess. Yet, the path to this promised land is strewn with challenges – from the technical to the cultural. Businesses poised to make this transition must first take stock of their readiness, navigating a landscape marked by opportunities and pitfalls.

ASSESSING YOUR AI READINESS: A CHECKLIST FOR BUSINESSES

Evaluating Current Systems

The first step in this assessment is akin to holding a mirror to the organization's existing systems and processes, seeking reflections of both strength and vulnerability. This evaluation must extend beyond the immediate technological infrastructure to encompass data management practices, software compatibility, and the scalability of current systems. Businesses need to question not if their systems can accommodate AI but whether they can do so in a manner that amplifies AI's potential. For instance, an e-commerce platform looking to implement AI for personalized recommendations must evaluate the robustness of its website infrastructure and the comprehensiveness of its customer data collection practices.

Identifying Gaps and Opportunities

This phase requires a keen eye for both the overt and the hidden, identifying gaps hindering AI integration and opportunities that AI could uniquely fill. For example, a manufacturing company might discover a gap in real-time data collection from its machinery, a crucial input for AI-driven predictive maintenance. Conversely, the same company might identify an opportunity to leverage AI to optimize its supply chain, reducing waste and improving efficiency. This identification process goes beyond mere listing; it demands strategic prioritization, focusing on areas where AI can deliver the most significant impact in alignment with business goals.

Technical and Cultural Readiness

Technical readiness, while critical, forms only one-half of the equation. The other, equally vital, is cultural readiness — an organization's capability to embrace change, foster innovation, and adapt to new working methods. This extends from the C-suite to the front lines, necessitating a culture where AI is viewed not with apprehension but as a tool for empowerment. A business might have the most advanced technological setup, but without a workforce that is curious, adaptable, and skilled in leveraging AI, the technology risks remaining underutilized. Preparing for AI integration thus requires parallel tracks: upgrading technical infrastructure and nurturing a culture conducive to innovation.

Preparation Strategies

Preparation for AI integration is multifaceted, demanding a strategic approach to technological upgrades and staff training. On the technical front, businesses might need to invest in cloud computing solutions to ensure scalability, enhance their data analytics capabilities, or adopt modular software architectures that can easily integrate AI functionalities. Concurrently, staff training programs must be instituted to enhance technical skills and foster an understanding of AI's strategic value and ethical considerations. This dual approach ensures that when AI is introduced, the organization is not scrambling to catch up but is ready to hit the ground running.

Visual Element: AI Readiness Interactive Checklist

An interactive checklist is provided to aid businesses in this critical assessment phase, encompassing key areas such as technical infrastructure, data management practices, staff skills, and organizational culture. This tool allows businesses to methodically evaluate their AI readiness, highlighting areas of strength and pinpointing those requiring attention. It serves as a diagnostic instrument and a planning guide, ensuring businesses approach AI integration with clarity and strategic focus.

In navigating the complex terrain of AI integration, businesses are called to embark on a journey that is as much about technological enhancement as it is about cultural transformation. Assessing AI readiness, spanning technical systems, organizational culture, and strategic alignment, lays the groundwork for this profound change. It is a process that demands honesty, strategic foresight, and a commitment to continuous improvement. With a clear understanding of their current state and a roadmap for preparation, businesses can move forward confidently, ready to harness AI's transformative potential to its fullest.

OVERCOMING INTEGRATION CHALLENGES: STRATEGIES AND SOLUTIONS

Integrating Artificial Intelligence (AI) into existing systems represents a significant endeavor for businesses, marked by a complex interplay of technical, organizational, and operational challenges. This intricate process demands technological insight, strategic foresight, and collaborative synergy. Amidst this landscape, several hurdles persistently emerge, posing substantial obstacles to seamless AI integration. Yet, with a nuanced understanding of these challenges and a repertoire of strategic responses, businesses can navigate these hurdles adeptly, paving the way for AI to redefine their operational paradigms.

Common Integration Challenges

A recurrent challenge in AI integration lies in the discordance between existing IT infrastructures and the novel demands of AI technologies. Legacy systems, often rigid and siloed, can clash with AI applications' dynamic, data-intensive nature. This discordance can stifle data flow, which is crucial for feeding AI algorithms, leading to bottlenecks that impede AI functionality. Additionally, the scarcity of AI expertise within organizations compounds integration difficulties, leaving businesses grappling with the intricacies of AI without adequate internal guidance. These challenges and concerns over data privacy, security, and regulatory compliance create a multifaceted obstacle course that businesses must navigate to unlock AI's potential.

Custom Solutions vs. Off-the-Shelf Products

The dichotomy between custom AI solutions and off-the-shelf AI products presents businesses with a strategic choice, each with distinct advantages and limitations. Custom AI solutions, tailored to a business's specific needs and operational nuances, offer unparalleled alignment with organizational goals. However, developing bespoke AI systems demands substantial investment in time, capital, and expertise, posing a significant barrier for many organizations. Conversely, off-the-shelf AI products provide a more accessible entry point to AI integration, offering ready-made solutions that can be swiftly deployed. Yet, this convenience often comes at the cost of flexibility, as these products may only partially align with the unique requirements of the business, necessitating adjustments that can dilute their effectiveness.

Cross-Departmental Collaboration

The successful integration of AI into business operations hinges on the collaboration between IT departments, operational units, and other organizational divisions. This collaborative effort ensures a holistic approach to AI integration, where operational insights and vice versa inform technological implementations. For instance, IT specialists, with their deep understanding of AI technologies, can work alongside operational teams to identify use cases where AI can drive significant improvements. This synergy accelerates the integration process and fosters a shared sense of ownership and enthusiasm for AI initiatives across the organization. Moreover, promoting collaboration across departments mitigates the risk of resistance to AI integration, as it ensures all stakeholders have a voice in the process, aligning AI strategies with the broader organizational vision.

Case Studies

A compelling illustration of overcoming AI integration challenges is found in a multinational retail corporation that embarked on an ambitious journey to embed AI across its operations. Faced with a legacy IT infrastructure ill-suited for AI's data demands, the company initiated a comprehensive digital transformation program. This program, characterized by the modernization of its IT environment and the adoption of cloud computing solutions, laid the groundwork for AI integration. Collaborative workshops, bringing together IT professionals and retail managers, facilitated a mutual understanding of AI's operational potential and technical requirements. This collaborative endeavor led to successfully deploying AI-driven inventory management systems and customer service chatbots, significantly enhancing operational efficiency and customer satisfaction.

Another example is a healthcare provider that leveraged AI to improve patient care and operational efficiency. Initial attempts at AI integration were met with significant challenges, including data silo issues and a lack of AI literacy among staff. Through strategic partnerships with AI technology firms and a dedicated program for staff training and engagement, the healthcare provider surmounted these obstacles. The result was the successful implementation of AI-driven diagnostic tools and patient management systems, markedly improving patient outcomes and operational workflows.

In navigating the challenges of AI integration, businesses uncover a landscape where obstacles coexist with opportunities. By recognizing and strategically addressing common integration challenges, choosing between custom solutions and off-the-shelf products with discernment, fostering cross-departmental collaboration, and drawing inspiration from real-world case studies, organizations can adeptly integrate AI into their operations. Though fraught with complexity, this journey promises to redefine businesses in profound ways, ushering in an era of enhanced efficiency, innovation, and competitiveness.

ENSURING COMPATIBILITY: AI AND LEGACY SYSTEMS

The interplay between burgeoning AI technologies and entrenched legacy systems presents a formidable challenge for businesses navigating digital transformation. Legacy systems, characterized by their robust yet rigid architectures, are testaments to an organization's historical growth and operational strategies. However, as the digital dawn beckons, these systems often emerge as relics ill-suited to AI integration's dynamic, data-driven demands. This discord between the old and the new necessitates a nuanced approach, where strategies and technologies are employed not merely to bridge but to synergize the capabilities of both worlds, ensuring a seamless melding of tradition and innovation.

The Legacy System Dilemma

The crux of the challenge with legacy systems lies in their inherent limitations—architectural rigidity, outdated interfaces, and siloed data structures—that starkly contrast with AI technologies' fluid, interconnected nature. While reliable for specific, unchanging tasks, these systems falter under the weight of AI's need for real-time data access, scalable computing resources, and agile methodologies. Organizations find themselves at a crossroads, where the path forward demands not only technological upgrades but a reimagining of operational paradigms to accommodate the transformative potential of AI.

The strategy to address these challenges begins with a meticulous audit and a thorough examination of existing systems to identify bottlenecks, compatibility issues, and areas where AI can deliver immediate value. This audit, coupled with stakeholder consultations, sheds light on the operational impact of potential AI integrations, paving the way for informed decision-making. The goal is to devise a roadmap that acknowledges the constraints of legacy systems while leveraging their stable, tried-and-tested functionalities as a foundation for AI-driven enhancements.

Bridging Technologies

Emerging technologies and approaches offer a lifeline, enabling businesses to weave AI capabilities into the fabric of their legacy systems. Middleware solutions, for instance, serve as conduits, facilitating communication and data exchange between disparate systems and AI applications. These software layers abstract the complexity of underlying systems, providing a unified interface for AI tools to interact with existing databases, applications, and services. Similarly, APIs (Application Programming Interfaces) emerge as versatile tools, enabling modular connections that extend the functionality of legacy systems with AI-driven capabilities. Through these bridging technologies, businesses can incrementally infuse AI into their operations, mitigating compatibility issues while capitalizing on the strengths of their existing infrastructures.

Incremental Integration

The path to harmonizing AI with legacy systems is best navigated through an incremental approach, a strategy that mitigates disruption while allowing for continuous adaptation. This methodology advocates for the phased introduction of AI applications, starting with low-risk, high-impact areas that can provide immediate benefits and serve as proof of concept. Each phase involves targeted deployments, rigorous testing, and feedback loops, ensuring that each integration is optimized for performance and compatibility. This step-wise progression allows organizations to adjust their strategies in response to technological advancements, operational feedback, and evolving business needs. It transforms the integration process into a dynamic, iterative journey where learning and adaptation are constant companions.

Success Stories

Amid the theoretical and strategic discourse, real-world success stories offer concrete examples of how businesses have effectively integrated AI with their legacy systems. A prominent financial institution grappling with the limitations of its legacy banking platform embarked on an ambitious project to enhance customer service through AI-driven chatbots and personalized financial advice. Leveraging middleware to connect its AI applications with the existing customer database, the bank succeeded in delivering real-time, personalized services, significantly improving customer satisfaction and operational efficiency.

Another illustrative case involves a logistics company facing the challenge of optimizing its sprawling global supply chain, which is managed by a patchwork of legacy systems. The company achieved unprecedented visibility into its operations by adopting APIs to integrate AI-driven analytics and forecasting tools. This integration enabled predictive modeling of supply chain disruptions, optimized routing, and inventory management, yielding substantial cost savings and improved service levels.

These narratives underscore a critical insight: integrating AI with legacy systems is not merely a technological challenge but an opportunity for business transformation. Through strategic planning, the deployment of bridging technologies, and an incremental approach to integration, businesses can unlock the latent potential of their legacy systems, propelling them into a future where tradition and innovation merge to create new value. In this journey, the legacy system dilemma evolves from a barrier to a catalyst, driving businesses towards operational excellence and competitive advantage in the digital age.

MITIGATING DISRUPTION: KEEPING YOUR BUSINESS RUNNING SMOOTHLY

In the intricate dance of weaving Artificial Intelligence (AI) into the operational tapestry of a business, a critical challenge that leaders must navigate is the potential disruption to ongoing operations. If not carefully managed, this disruption can ripple through the organization, affecting productivity, employee morale, and customer satisfaction. Hence, integrating AI into business processes demands a meticulous strategy that not only anticipates potential disruptions but also puts measures to mitigate them in place, ensuring the business remains resilient and functional throughout the transition.

Planning for Continuity

A cornerstone of this strategy is a robust plan for business continuity that acts as a bulwark against the possible upheavals brought about by AI integration. This plan starts with a thorough risk assessment, identifying areas where AI implementation might intersect critically with day-to-day operations. For instance, integrating AI into a customer service platform requires understanding how this might affect response times or issue resolution during the transition phase. This assessment develops contingency plans detailing alternative workflows, temporary manual processes, or fallback systems that can be activated should AI integration face unexpected hurdles. Additionally, this planning phase involves clear communication channels, ensuring that all stakeholders, from employees to customers, are informed about the potential for disruption and the steps to minimize it. This transparency prepares them for what's ahead and builds trust in the organization's capacity to manage change.

Employee Engagement and Training

At the heart of successful AI integration lies the engagement and training of employees, transforming potential disruptors into champions of change. This engagement is twofold; first, it involves creating awareness about the benefits and challenges of

AI, dispelling myths, and setting realistic expectations. This is achieved through workshops, seminars, and regular updates informing the workforce about the AI projects underway and their anticipated impact. Second, training programs are crucial, equipping employees with the skills and knowledge necessary to adapt to new AI-enhanced workflows. These programs must be tailored, recognizing the varied levels of technological proficiency across the workforce. For roles significantly affected by AI, hands-on training with the new systems, guided by AI experts, can facilitate a smoother transition. Moreover, creating internal AI mentors or champions can help sustain ongoing learning and adaptation, providing a peer resource for employees navigating the new landscape.

Monitoring and Feedback Loops

An agile approach to AI integration emphasizes the importance of real-time monitoring and feedback loops. This approach involves setting up systems that can track the performance of AI applications and their impact on operations from day one. Dashboards that provide a live view of critical metrics related to AI functionality, employee productivity, and customer satisfaction become invaluable. These monitoring tools must be complemented by feedback mechanisms where employees can report issues, suggest improvements, or share insights on how AI affects their work. This feedback, collected through surveys, suggestion boxes, or digital platforms, offers a direct line into the workforce's experience, allowing for quick identification of problems and opportunities for refinement. Actively responding to this feedback not only aids in fine-tuning AI applications but also fosters a culture of continuous improvement and inclusivity.

Flexible Implementation Plans

Flexibility in the implementation plans for AI projects is not merely a virtue but a necessity. This flexibility allows for adjusting project timelines, scope, and methodologies in response to emerging challenges, technological developments, or shifts in business priorities. It involves creating modular implementation roadmaps, where AI projects are broken down into smaller, manageable phases. This modular approach facilitates easier monitoring and adjustment and enables quick wins that can build momentum and support for the AI initiative. Furthermore, flexibility entails having a diversified portfolio of AI projects, balancing between high-risk, high-reward projects and those with guaranteed short-term benefits. This diversification ensures that even as some projects may face delays or challenges, others can continue to deliver value, maintaining a positive trajectory for the overall AI integration effort.

In navigating the complexities of AI integration, businesses confront the dual challenge of harnessing AI's transformative potential while ensuring the smooth running of day-to-day operations. The strategies outlined here, from robust planning for business continuity and comprehensive employee engagement to agile monitoring and feedback mechanisms, offer a blueprint for mitigating disruption. By embedding these strategies into the fabric of AI integration efforts, businesses can move forward confidently, poised to unlock the myriad benefits of AI without sacrificing operational integrity or stakeholder trust.

CASE STUDY: SUCCESSFUL AI INTEGRATION IN RETAIL

In the competitive retail arena, a mid-sized company known for its eclectic mix of products and personalized customer service faced the pressing need to innovate or risk obsolescence. The leadership recognized that artificial intelligence (AI) held the key to streamlining operations and elevating the customer experience to new heights. Their objective was clear: integrate AI across the spectrum of their operations, from inventory management to customer service, without losing the personal touch that distinguished them in the market.

The endeavor had its challenges. Initially, the existing IT infrastructure needed improvement, but it struggled to support the data-intensive demands of AI algorithms. Additionally, the workforce, though skilled in traditional retail operations, was largely unversed in AI, viewing it with a mix of apprehension and skepticism. These challenges were compounded by concerns about maintaining the company's hallmark personalized customer service in the face of automation.

The solutions implemented were multifaceted and inventive. The company upgraded its IT infrastructure, adopting cloud services to ensure scalability and investing in robust data analytics platforms. Parallel to these technological upgrades, a comprehensive training program was rolled out, designed to demystify AI for the workforce and highlight its potential to enhance, rather than replace, human capabilities. To address the challenge of preserving personalized customer service, the company developed an AI system capable of learning from customer interactions, thereby enabling a previously unattainable personalization level.

The outcomes of these efforts were transformative. Once a painstaking process prone to errors and inefficiencies, inventory management was revolutionized through AI-driven predictive analytics, leading to significant reductions in overstock and stockouts. Meanwhile, the AI-enhanced customer service platform provided customers personalized recommendations and support, increasing customer satisfaction and loyalty. Perhaps most notably, the integration of AI freed employees from mundane tasks, allowing them to focus on what they did best: creating unique and memorable customer experiences.

From this case study, several key learnings emerged:

1. It is important to view AI not as a panacea but as a tool that, when thoughtfully integrated, can significantly amplify a company's strengths.
2. The critical role of workforce engagement and training in successfully adopting AI underscores that technological innovation must go hand in hand with human capital development.
3. A strategic, phased approach to technology upgrades is necessary to ensure that the infrastructure evolves in tandem with the company's AI ambitions.
4. AI has the potential to enhance operational efficiency and elevate the customer experience in previously unimaginable ways.

This narrative serves as a testament to AI's transformative potential in the retail sector, offering valuable insights and best practices for businesses embarking on their own AI integration journeys. It underscores AI's power to redefine not only how businesses operate but also how they engage with their customers, promising a future where personalized service and operational excellence go hand in hand.

As we close this chapter, it becomes evident that integrating AI into business operations is not merely a technological endeavor but a strategic one, requiring careful planning, a commitment to training and development, and a clear vision of the desired outcomes. The retail company's journey illustrates how AI, when strategically integrated, can significantly enhance efficiency, customer satisfaction, and innovation. This case study sheds light on the challenges and solutions inherent in AI integration and highlights the broader implications for businesses seeking to navigate the digital transformation landscape. With these insights in mind, we move forward, exploring how AI reshapes operations and redefines the essence of customer engagement and service excellence.

UNLOCKING THE AI-DRIVEN CUSTOMER EXPERIENCE

In the complex realm of modern business, where each interaction can shape the course of brand loyalty, Artificial Intelligence (AI) emerges as the guiding thread, empowering companies to navigate the intricacies of personalized customer experiences. This chapter emphasizes how AI, far from being an esoteric tool, acts as a bridge connecting the vast expanse between data and personal touch, transforming how businesses understand, engage, and delight their customers.

ENHANCING CUSTOMER EXPERIENCES WITH AI

Personalization at Scale

Imagine walking into a café where the barista, without prompting, starts preparing your favorite blend when you enter the door. This level of personalization, a hallmark of small-town shops, is now scalable to the global stage through AI. By analyzing customer data points—past purchases, preferences, and even social media activity—AI simultaneously crafts individualized experiences for millions. By leveraging this capability, online retailers present product recommendations that resonate personally with each visitor, significantly enhancing the shopping experience and boosting conversion rates. This isn't just about selling more; it's about creating a sense of connection and understanding, akin to the barista who knows your order by heart.

AI in Customer Service

Once fraught with long wait times and scripted responses, the domain of customer service is undergoing a renaissance with AI-powered chatbots and virtual assistants. These AI entities are available 24/7, providing instant responses to customer inquiries, from tracking orders to resolving common issues, all conversationally mimicking human interaction. Beyond the immediate benefit of reduced wait times, these AI solutions offer a consistently positive experience crucial for building trust and loyalty. Moreover, they free human agents to tackle more complex, nuanced customer concerns, ensuring that when a human touch is needed, it receives the full attention it deserves.

Predictive Analytics for Customer Insights

With predictive analytics, businesses can anticipate customer needs before explicitly expressing them. This branch of AI analyzes patterns in customer behavior to forecast future actions, enabling companies to proactively offer products, services, or information that meet emerging demands. For instance, a streaming service might use predictive analytics to suggest shows a viewer is likely to enjoy based on their watching history. This proactive approach elevates the customer experience by making it effortlessly seamless and engenders a deep sense of being understood and valued on an individual level.

Success Stories

Let's take a look at some real-world success stories. A global e-commerce giant, by integrating AI, achieved unprecedented levels of personalization and efficiency. Customers received product recommendations so tailored it felt like the website could read their minds, leading to record-breaking sales and customer satisfaction scores. Similarly, a telecommunications company implemented AI in its customer service operations, reducing response times to under a minute and solving over 90% of issues on the first contact. These stories are not just about AI's potential; they are about its proven ability to exceed customer expectations and set new standards for excellence in customer service.

Visual Element: Chart of AI's Impact on Customer Satisfaction

A comprehensive chart illustrates the tangible benefits of AI integration in customer-facing operations. It contrasts key metrics such as response time, issue resolution rate, and customer satisfaction before and after AI adoption. This visual representation highlights the significant improvements AI brings to customer experiences and serves as a compelling argument for its strategic integration into customer service models.

In navigating the intricate dance of modern customer engagement, businesses find AI an invaluable partner that brings the precision of data and the intuition of personal connection into a harmonious balance. From crafting personalized experiences at an unimaginable scale to revolutionizing customer service with efficiency and empathy, AI stands as a testament to the transformative power of technology when wielded with insight and strategic foresight. Through these AI-driven initiatives, businesses not only cater to their customers' evolving expectations but also pave the way for new paradigms of customer experience, where every interaction is an opportunity to delight and every engagement a step towards enduring loyalty.

STREAMLINING OPERATIONS: AI IN SUPPLY CHAIN MANAGEMENT

In the complex world of global commerce, the supply chain is the backbone, demanding precision, efficiency, and adaptability. The infusion of AI into this critical arena marks a pivotal shift, transforming supply chains from rigid, linear systems into dynamic, responsive webs. This is not just an incremental change; it's a fundamental reimagining of how goods are moved, stored, and delivered. AI ensures that the right products reach the right destinations at the right times with unprecedented efficiency, reshaping traditional business models and setting new standards for supply chain management.

AI for Efficient Supply Chains

At the core of AI's transformative impact on supply chains is its ability to sift through vast oceans of data, identify patterns, predict outcomes, and make decisions with a speed and accuracy that surpasses human capability. This capability is crucial in a domain where timing is everything, and the cost of delays or missteps can have profound economic implications. AI algorithms, trained on historical data and real-time inputs, can anticipate fluctuations in demand, identify potential bottlenecks before they occur, and suggest optimal routes for transportation, all in the pursuit of a singular goal: the seamless flow of goods from origin to consumer. The result is a supply chain that is not only more efficient but also more resilient, capable of adapting to disruptions ranging from sudden shifts in consumer demand to unforeseen global events.

Predictive Maintenance

One of the most tangible benefits of AI in supply chain management is its role in predictive maintenance. This proactive approach, in contrast to the traditional reactive model, can significantly reduce downtime and extend the lifespan of equipment. AI, by continuously monitoring the condition of machinery and vehicles, can predict failures before they occur, scheduling maintenance during off-peak hours and ensuring that the machinery is operational when needed most. This not only reduces operational costs and increases productivity but also ensures that the supply chain maintains its pulse even in the face of potential disruptions, demonstrating the transformative power of AI in supply chain management.

Inventory Management

The art of inventory management, balancing the scales between excess and inadequacy, finds a powerful ally in AI. Traditional inventory practices, often reliant on heuristic rules or simplistic forecasting models, need help accommodating modern consumer demand's complexities, leading to overstocking, stockouts, and lost sales. AI revolutionizes this domain through advanced analytics and machine learning models that can accurately forecast demand across multiple channels, considering factors ranging from seasonal trends to promotional activities. Moreover, AI systems can dynamically adjust inventory levels in real time, responding to actual sales data and market signals with a precision that manual processes cannot match. This dynamic inventory management approach optimizes stock levels and enhances order accuracy, ensuring that businesses can meet customer needs without the burden of excess inventory tying up capital.

Case Studies

The practical application of AI in supply chain management is best illustrated through real-world examples highlighting the challenges encountered and the solutions devised. A notable case involves a multinational manufacturing firm grappling with the dual challenges of maintaining high service levels while minimizing inventory costs. The firm implemented an AI-driven platform that integrated data from across its global supply chain, applying machine learning algorithms to forecast demand with high accuracy. The result was a dramatic reduction in inventory levels, freeing up millions in previously tied-up capital without compromising service levels.

Another compelling example is a leading logistics company facing the challenge of optimizing its delivery routes in the face of fluctuating demand and unpredictable disruptions. By leveraging AI to analyze real-time traffic data, weather reports, and historical delivery performance, the company could adjust its delivery routes dynamically, reducing fuel costs and improving on-time delivery rates. The AI system also recommended adjustments to loading strategies, further enhancing efficiency and reducing the environmental impact of delivery operations.

These case studies underscore the multifaceted benefits of AI in supply chain management, from predictive maintenance and dynamic inventory management to route optimization and beyond. They highlight how AI, through its ability to analyze data, predict outcomes, and recommend actions, can transform supply chains into agile, efficient entities that respond to the current landscape and anticipate future trends and disruptions. This transformation, underpinned by AI, ensures that supply chains can support the demands of modern commerce, delivering products and services with a level of efficiency and responsiveness that sets new benchmarks for operational excellence.

AI-DRIVEN DECISION MAKING: TRANSFORMING LEADERSHIP

In the realm of Leadership, where decisions shape the futures of companies and the destinies of their stakeholders, Artificial Intelligence (AI) emerges as a pivotal force. It equips leaders with the tools to navigate the complexities of the modern business landscape through informed, data-driven decision-making processes. This profound transformation marks a shift from intuition-based to evidence-based strategies that can significantly enhance operational effectiveness and strategic planning.

Data-Driven Decisions

AI redefines the contours of leadership decision-making by embedding a culture of precision and rationality into the decision-making process. In this new paradigm, leaders leverage AI to sift through the vast expanses of data, extracting actionable insights that inform strategic decisions. This capability is far from trivial; it represents a monumental shift in decisions, moving away from gut feelings and towards a model where data substantiate choices. For instance, marketing strategies that were once based on broad demographic assumptions can now be refined and targeted using AI's analysis of consumer behavior patterns, leading to campaigns that are not only more effective but also more cost-efficient. This approach upholds the role of human judgment; it augments it, providing leaders with a comprehensive view of the variables at play and enabling more nuanced and effective decision-making.

Risk Assessment

The dynamic nature of today's business environment, fraught with uncertainties and unpredictable variables, demands a proactive stance on risk management. AI tools are indispensable, allowing leaders to assess risks in real-time and adapt strategies accordingly. Through predictive analytics and machine learning algorithms, these tools can identify potential threats and vulnerabilities, from market fluctuations to operational risks, with a degree of accuracy and speed unattainable through traditional methods. Moreover, AI's capacity to simulate various scenarios and their outcomes allows leaders to evaluate the potential impacts of their decisions, ensuring that risk management is an integral part of the strategic planning process. This real-time, predictive approach to risk assessment empowers leaders to make informed decisions that safeguard their organizations against potential pitfalls, ensuring resilience and stability in the face of adversity.

Scenario Planning

In the intricate tapestry of business strategy, scenario planning is a crucial thread, enabling organizations to prepare for many future possibilities. AI significantly enhances this planning process, offering leaders the tools to create and analyze scenarios based on varying assumptions and variables. Through the integration of AI, scenario planning transcends its traditional boundaries, leveraging algorithms to process vast datasets and generate predictive models that illuminate potential futures. This capability allows leaders to envision different scenarios and quantify their impacts, providing a data-driven foundation for strategic flexibility and adaptability. For example, an organization considering expanding into a new market can use AI to simulate various entry strategies, evaluating each against various economic, competitive, and regulatory factors. This informed approach to scenario planning ensures that organizations are not merely reactive to changes but are proactively prepared with strategies that are robust, flexible, and grounded in data-driven insights.

Leadership Insights

The testament to AI's transformative impact on leadership decision-making is most vividly seen in the reflections of leaders who have embraced this paradigm shift. These leaders recount a transition from ambiguity to clarity, where decision-making processes are no longer clouded by uncertainty but are illuminated by data-driven insights. They speak of the empowerment that comes from having access to real-time data and analytics, which enables them to make informed decisions swiftly, keeping their organizations agile and competitive. Moreover, they highlight the role of AI in democratizing decision-making, where insights are not confined to the upper echelons of Leadership but are accessible across the organization, fostering a culture of informed participation and strategic alignment. These reflections underscore a critical realization: AI, as a facilitator of data-driven decision-making, is not merely a technological tool but a strategic asset redefining Leadership in the digital age.

In this time of unprecedented complexity and change, AI-driven decision-making emerges as an option and an imperative for leaders seeking to navigate the challenges and opportunities of the business landscape. Through the infusion of data-driven insights, real-time risk assessment, and enhanced scenario planning, AI equips leaders with the tools to make decisions that are not only informed but also strategic, adaptive, and aligned with the long-term vision of their organizations. While rooted in technology, this transformation extends beyond it, heralding a new age of Leadership defined by precision, foresight, and a deep commitment to informed strategy.

INNOVATING PRODUCTS AND SERVICES THROUGH AI INSIGHTS

In the crucible of market competition, where differentiation is the linchpin of survival and growth, Artificial Intelligence (AI) emerges as a potent catalyst, propelling organizations toward the frontier of innovation. When harnessed with strategic intent, this transformative force amplifies product and service innovation capacity. It redefines development paradigms, bringing solutions that align with the evolving tapestry of customer needs and expectations.

Leveraging AI for Innovation

At the confluence of data analytics and machine learning, AI unveils a vista of untapped opportunities, guiding enterprises through the uncharted territories of innovation. This journey begins with extracting nuanced insights from layers of customer data, discerning latent needs and emerging trends that remain invisible to the conventional eye. With these insights, organizations can pioneer novel products and services or enhance existing offerings with features that resonate personally with their target audience. For instance, AI's ability to analyze social media sentiment and online behavior patterns can illuminate unmet customer desires, inspiring the creation of products that fill these gaps, thereby addressing market voids with precision and agility.

Customer-Centric Development

The ethos of customer-centricity, long heralded as a cornerstone of successful product development, finds a new champion in AI. AI transforms customer-centricity from a guiding principle into an actionable strategy through its unparalleled data analysis capacity. This transformation is rooted in AI's ability to dissect vast datasets, extracting actionable insights that inform every stage of the product development process. From conceptualization to design, companies can leverage AI to ensure that customer preferences and feedback are integral to product evolution, resulting in offerings that meet and anticipate customer needs. This approach elevates the relevance and appeal of products and fosters a deeper connection with customers, cultivating loyalty and advocacy.

Speed to Market

In the relentless race to capture market share, the velocity at which products move from ideation to launch emerges as a critical determinant of success. Herein lies another facet of AI's transformative impact: its role in compressing development cycles and expediting time to market. By automating aspects of the design and testing phases, AI significantly reduces the time required to refine prototypes and validate product concepts. Furthermore, predictive analytics, a subset of AI, offers foresight into potential market shifts and customer reactions, allowing companies to adjust their development strategies proactively. This acceleration of the development process does not sacrifice quality for speed; instead, it ensures that products are rapidly deployed and deeply aligned with market demands, a dual achievement that positions companies favorably in the eyes of consumers and investors alike.

Innovation Case Studies

The tangible impact of AI on product and service innovation is vividly illustrated in the successes of companies that have embraced its potential. One example is a technology firm that leveraged AI to revolutionize personal fitness devices. Through continuous analysis of user data, the firm identified a growing demand for holistic health tracking beyond mere physical activity. In response, it developed a new wearable device that monitors physical parameters and tracks mental well-being, using AI to provide personalized health insights and recommendations. This innovation, rooted in AI-derived customer insights, captured a sizable market segment and set new industry standards for health and fitness tracking.

Another example is a financial services company that utilized AI to transform the customer banking experience. Recognizing the growing demand for personalized financial advice, the company deployed AI algorithms to analyze customer data, including spending habits, financial goals, and risk tolerance. Based on this analysis, it launched a suite of personalized banking services, offering customers customized investment recommendations, budgeting advice, and financial planning tools. This AI-driven innovation enhanced customer satisfaction and loyalty and positioned the company as a leader in personalized financial services, demonstrating the profound impact of AI on service innovation.

In the dynamic product and service development arena, AI emerges as a formidable force, driving innovation with insights gleaned from the depths of data and accelerating the journey from concept to market. Through its capacity to unlock new opportunities, ensure customer-centric development, and expedite time to market, AI redefines the landscape of innovation, offering companies a strategic advantage in their quest to meet and surpass customer expectations. In this era of rapid technological advancement and shifting consumer preferences, AI stands as a beacon of innovation, guiding companies toward creating products and services that resonate with customers and herald new paradigms of excellence and engagement.

ACHIEVING OPERATIONAL EXCELLENCE WITH PREDICTIVE ANALYTICS

Optimizing Operations

In the vast expanse of modern business operations, predictive analytics stands as a beacon, guiding entities toward realms of efficiency and cost-effectiveness previously deemed unreachable. This facet of artificial intelligence, intricate in its capacity to sift through and make sense of vast datasets, offers a predictive lens through which businesses can glimpse the future of their operations. By meticulously analyzing patterns and trends within operational data, predictive analytics provides actionable insights that enable enterprises to refine processes, reduce waste, and enhance productivity. For instance, a manufacturing firm might utilize predictive analytics to optimize its production schedules, ensuring machinery is utilized at peak efficiency while minimizing energy consumption. This strategic application streamlines operations and contributes to substantial cost savings, illustrating the profound impact of predictive analytics on operational optimization.

Forecasting Demand

The application of AI in forecasting demand represents a paradigm shift in how businesses anticipate market needs and align their operations accordingly. Through the meticulous analysis of historical sales data, market trends, and consumer behavior patterns, AI algorithms offer precise demand forecasts. These forecasts empower businesses to adjust their production, inventory, and distribution strategies proactively, ensuring they are primed to meet market demands without succumbing to the pitfalls of overproduction or stock shortages. A retail chain, for instance, might leverage AI to predict seasonal fluctuations in product demand, enabling it to adjust its inventory levels dynamically. This precision in forecasting ensures optimal stock levels and enhances customer satisfaction by guaranteeing product availability, showcasing the instrumental role of AI in harmonizing operations with market dynamics.

Quality Control

The sphere of quality control, critical to sustaining brand reputation and customer trust, has been invigorated through the integration of AI's advanced analytics and real-time monitoring capabilities. By continuously analyzing production data and employing machine learning algorithms, AI systems can detect deviations from quality standards with unprecedented accuracy and speed. This capability allows for the immediate rectification of issues before they escalate, significantly reducing the incidence of defective products reaching the customer. Moreover, AI's role in quality control extends beyond detection to prevention, with predictive models identifying potential points of failure within the production process. This proactive approach to quality control elevates product standards and streamlines operations, reducing the time and resources traditionally allocated to quality assurance procedures.

Operational Excellence Examples

The tangible benefits of leveraging predictive analytics for operational excellence are best illuminated through the successes of businesses that have embraced this technology. One illustrative example is a logistics company that implemented predictive analytics to enhance its fleet management. By analyzing real-time and historical data on vehicle performance, traffic conditions, and delivery schedules, the company optimized its routes, reducing fuel consumption and improving delivery times. This strategic application of predictive analytics bolstered operational efficiency and contributed to environmental sustainability by minimizing the company's carbon footprint.

Another example is a food and beverage manufacturer that utilized AI to refine its quality control processes. By integrating real-time monitoring systems equipped with machine learning capabilities, the manufacturer could detect minute deviations in product quality, such as variations in packaging seal integrity. This immediate detection enabled swift corrective actions, significantly reducing product recall rates. The predictive aspect of the AI system also provided insights into the root causes of quality issues, allowing for process adjustments that preemptively mitigated future occurrences. This holistic approach to quality control, underpinned by AI, exemplifies the profound impact of predictive analytics on achieving operational excellence, setting a benchmark for quality and efficiency within the industry.

In the intricate dance of modern business operations, the strategic application of predictive analytics emerges as a critical choreography, orchestrating a symphony of efficiency, precision, and innovation. Through the optimization of operations, accurate forecasting of demand, and enhancement of quality control processes, businesses unlock new dimensions of operational excellence, propelled by the foresight and agility afforded by AI. This journey towards operational mastery, guided by the insights and capabilities of predictive analytics, not only fortifies businesses against the vicissitudes of market dynamics but also paves the way for sustainable growth and competitive advantage.

As we navigate the evolving landscapes of business and technology, the role of AI, particularly predictive analytics, in driving operational excellence offers a compelling narrative of transformation. This chapter has elucidated the multifaceted impact of AI on refining operations, from optimizing production lines to ensuring quality control and aligning with market demand. These advancements, emblematic of the broader shift towards data-driven decision-making and strategic agility, herald a new era of operational efficiency that transcends traditional boundaries. As we venture forth, the integration of AI across business functions continues to unfold, promising enhancements in operational efficiency and a redefinition of what it means to excel in the modern business environment.

UNDERSTANDING GENERATIVE AI FOR BUSINESS LEADERS

DEMYSTIFYING STRATEGIC ADVANTAGE, ETHICAL DEPLOYMENT, AND PRACTICAL INTERGRATION FOR SUCCESS

"Great leaders don't set out to be leaders. They set out to make a difference. It's never about the role—it's always about the goal."

— LISA HAISHA

People who give without expectation live longer, happier lives and make more money. So if we've got a shot at that during our time together, darn it, I'm gonna try.

To make that happen, I have a question for you…

Would you help someone you've never met, even if you never got credit for it?

Who is this person you ask? They are like you. Or, at least, like you used to be. Less experienced, wanting to make a difference, and needing help, but not sure where to look.

Our mission is to make Understanding Generative AI for Business Leaders accessible to everyone. Everything we do stems from that mission. And, the only way for us to accomplish that mission is by reaching…well…everyone.

This is where you come in. Most people do, in fact, judge a book by its cover (and its reviews). So here's my ask on behalf of a struggling business leader you've never met:

Please help that business leader by leaving this book a review.

Your gift costs no money and less than 60 seconds to make real, but can change a fellow business leaders life forever. Your review could help…

…one more small businesses provide for their community.

…one more entrepreneur support their family.

…one more employee get meaningful work.

..one more client transform their life.

…one more dream come true.

To get that 'feel good' feeling and help this person for real, all you have to do is…and it takes less than 60 seconds…

leave a review.

Simply scan the QR code below to leave your review:

If you feel good about helping a faceless Business Leader, you are my kind of person. Welcome to club. You're one of us.

I'm that much more excited to help you [ACHIEVE TARGET OUTCOMES] [FASTER/EASIER/MORE] than you can possibly imagine. You'll love the [TACTICS/LESSONS/STRATEGIES] I'm about to share in the coming chapters.

Thank you from the bottom of my heart. Now, back to our regularly scheduled program-ming.

- Your biggest fan, Synergy AI Editions

PS - Fun fact: If you provide something of value to another person, it makes you more valuable to them. If you'd like goodwill straight from another Business Leader - and you believe this book will help them - send this book their way.

SCAN ME

NAVIGATING THE ETHICAL TERRAIN OF AI

Within the tapestry of technological evolution, AI stands not as a mere thread but as a vibrant color, altering the pattern with each stroke of innovation. This vivid transformation, however, brings to light a spectrum of ethical considerations, painting a complex picture that demands meticulous attention. As businesses weave AI into the fabric of their operations, the brushstrokes of ethical decision-making become crucial in ensuring that the resulting picture aligns with societal values and norms. This chapter delves into creating an ethical AI framework, a structured approach to embedding ethical considerations into the lifecycle of AI projects. This ensures that these technologies serve as tools for enhancement rather than sources of contention.

ESTABLISHING AN ETHICAL AI FRAMEWORK

Defining Ethical Principles

At the foundation of any ethical AI framework lie the principles that guide its development and deployment. These principles, akin to the cardinal points on a compass, offer direction in navigating the ethical landscape of AI. They include fairness, ensuring that AI systems do not perpetuate discrimination; accountability, attributing responsibility for the outcomes of AI; transparency, making the workings of AI systems understandable to users; and privacy, safeguarding the personal information processed by AI technologies. For instance, the 'AI Fairness 360' toolkit developed by IBM Research is a practical example of how fairness can be embedded into AI systems. This toolkit provides a comprehensive set of metrics to check for bias in AI algorithms, enabling developers to ensure fairness in their models. Like a gardener who plants seeds with the hope of future blossoms, setting these principles at the inception of AI projects ensures that ethical considerations grow alongside technological advancements, deeply rooted in the lifecycle of every initiative.

Framework Implementation

The implementation of an ethical AI framework is analogous to constructing a building where the principles serve as the blueprint. This process begins with integrating ethical considerations into the initial design of AI technologies, ensuring that these systems are built with the capability to adhere to established ethical standards. It involves conducting impact assessments to identify potential ethical risks associated with the use of AI and developing proactive mitigation strategies. For instance, when designing an AI system for loan approval, incorporating mechanisms to regularly assess and adjust the algorithm for bias can prevent discriminatory practices. This proactive approach, which we strongly believe in, ensures that ethical considerations are not afterthoughts but integral components of the AI development process, giving you the confidence that we are actively working to address ethical concerns.

Stakeholder Engagement

The development of an ethical AI framework is not a solitary endeavor but a collaborative effort that involves engaging a broad spectrum of stakeholders, including policymakers. Policymakers play a crucial role in shaping the ethical landscape of AI, as they can enact laws and regulations that promote fairness, accountability, transparency, and privacy in AI development and deployment. This engagement is crucial in capturing diverse perspectives and values, ensuring that the framework reflects the multiplicity of societal norms and expectations. For example, convening focus groups with potential users of an AI-driven health diagnostic tool can provide insights into privacy concerns and expectations of transparency, guiding the development of ethical guidelines that resonate with those directly impacted by the technology. This inclusive approach not only enriches the ethical framework with a variety of viewpoints but also fosters a sense of shared responsibility and trust among all parties involved.

Continuous Evaluation

The landscape of technology and societal norms is in constant flux, necessitating the continuous evaluation and revision of ethical frameworks. This iterative process ensures that the guidelines governing AI's development and use remain relevant and effective in addressing emerging ethical challenges. It involves regular reviews of the ethical principles guiding AI projects and assessing their alignment with current societal values and technological capabilities. Moreover, this continuous evaluation benefits from incorporating feedback from users and stakeholders, offering a mechanism for adapting the ethical framework in response to practical experiences and concerns. Like a ship adjusting its sails to navigate changing winds, this process ensures that AI technologies remain aligned with ethical standards throughout their lifecycle, navigating evolving societal expectations and technological advancements.

Visual Element: Ethical AI Framework Checklist

This section includes a comprehensive checklist to facilitate implementing an ethical AI framework. This tool outlines key considerations and steps for embedding ethical principles into AI projects, from defining core values and conducting risk assessments to engaging stakeholders and establishing mechanisms for continuous evaluation. Each item on the checklist is accompanied by guiding questions and action points, offering a structured approach to navigating the ethical terrain of AI. This visual element serves as a resource for businesses embarking on the development of AI technologies and a reminder of the importance of ethical considerations in shaping the future of innovation.

The compass of ethics guides the journey in the realm of AI, where possibilities stretch as far as the imagination dares to venture. Establishing an ethical AI framework is a testament to the commitment to harnessing the power of technology for the greater good, ensuring that the advancements we celebrate today do not become the ethical quandaries of tomorrow.

ADDRESSING BIAS AND ENSURING FAIRNESS IN AI MODELS

In the nuanced world of artificial intelligence (AI), bias emerges as a silent architect, surreptitiously shaping outcomes that may not always align with the principles of fairness and equity. This section delves into the labyrinthine phenomenon of bias within AI systems, unraveling its origins, its ramifications for decision-making, and the concerted efforts required to cultivate models that embody fairness and impartiality.

Identifying Sources of Bias

Much like the shadowy figures in a chiaroscuro painting, bias in AI systems owes its existence to various sources, each contributing to the distortion of outcomes. At the heart of this issue lies the data used to train AI models. In its raw form, data reflects the world as it is, replete with historical inequities and societal prejudices that, when fed into AI systems, act as a template upon which biases are built and perpetuated. Another notable source is the algorithms that parse and learn from this data. These algorithms, designed by humans, are susceptible to the accidental infusion of the creators' biases, preferences, and blind spots, further complicating AI's bias landscape.

The impact of these biases extends far beyond the confines of the technical realm, seeping into the fabric of society, where they have the potential to amplify existing disparities. From financial services, where biased loan approval algorithms could reinforce economic disparities, to judicial systems, where predictive policing tools might disproportionately target certain demographics, the consequences of bias in AI are profound. For instance, if a facial recognition system is biased against a certain race, it could lead to wrongful arrests or exclusions from public spaces. This necessitates a robust framework for identification and mitigation to ensure that AI technologies are fair and equitable.

Mitigation Strategies

The commitment to fairness and equity in AI models is demonstrated through a proactive approach to addressing bias. This involves the adoption of algorithmic auditing, a comprehensive review process that scrutinizes AI models for bias and fairness across various dimensions. It includes examining the data and algorithms for inherent biases and testing the models in diverse scenarios to uncover any latent prejudices that might influence outcomes.

Another pivotal strategy revolves around the democratization of AI development, by fostering a diverse ecosystem of AI practitioners encompassing a wide array of backgrounds, perspectives, and disciplines, the likelihood of incorporating a broad spectrum of experiences and considerations into AI systems increases, thereby diluting the concentration of biases that might arise from a homogenous development team.

Diverse Data Sets

The cornerstone of any initiative to combat bias in AI lies in the meticulous curation of diverse, representative, and inclusive data sets. Though seemingly straightforward, this endeavor is fraught with challenges, demanding vigilance and a proactive stance in identifying and addressing gaps in data collection and annotation processes. By ensuring that the data encapsulates a broad spectrum of human experiences and conditions, the models trained on such data are better equipped to render fair and unbiased decisions.

A critical aspect of this process involves continuous monitoring and refinement of data sets. This task demands technical expertise and an acute awareness of the evolving dynamics of society and culture. This dynamic approach to data management ensures that AI models remain attuned to the nuances of fairness and equity, reflecting the changing contours of the world they are designed to serve.

Case Examples

The landscape of AI is dotted with instances that underscore the perils of bias and the endeavors to rectify these imbalances. One illustrative example involves a leading technology firm that grappled with the biases embedded within its facial recognition software. Initial iterations of the software exhibited a marked tendency to misidentify individuals from certain racial backgrounds, a discrepancy that stemmed from the lack of diversity in the training data. The firm's response involved overhauling its data collection processes, incorporating a more comprehensive array of images encompassing a broader spectrum of human features and skin tones. This recalibration enhanced the software's accuracy and served as a testament to the importance of diverse data sets in the quest for fairness in AI.

Another example is drawn from the realm of healthcare, where an AI tool designed to assist in treatment recommendations exhibited biases based on gender. The root of this bias was traced back to the historical data used to train the model, which disproportionately represented one gender. Recognizing the gravity of this oversight, the developers embarked on an initiative to rebalance the data, incorporating a more equitable distribution of gender-specific health data. This corrective measure mitigated the bias and underscored the critical role of continuous vigilance and adjustment in the pursuit of fairness in AI.

In the intricate dance of technology and ethics, eradicating bias from AI models emerges as a pivotal frontier, demanding a confluence of technical acumen, ethical foresight, and societal engagement. As we navigate this terrain, the commitment to fairness and equity in AI stands as a beacon, guiding our efforts to ensure that the advancements we herald today foster a world marked by justice and inclusivity for future generations.

PRIVACY AND DATA PROTECTION: AI'S ACHILLES' HEEL

In the intricate dance of innovation and privacy, artificial intelligence (AI) emerges as a double-edged sword, its sharpness honed by the data that feeds its insatiable appetite for learning and improvement—this reliance on vast personal information places AI at the epicenter of contemporary privacy and data protection debates. Here, the illumination of specific risks to privacy inherent in AI technologies becomes imperative, marking the terrain where the potential for misuse and violation of individual privacy rights shadows the promise of AI's capabilities.

Risks to Privacy

The essence of privacy risk in the context of AI pivots on the aggregation and analysis of personal data, activities that lie at the heart of AI's ability to learn, predict, and make autonomous decisions. While technologically remarkable, this process inherently raises concerns about the extent to which personal information is collected, stored, and utilized, often without explicit consent or awareness of the individuals involved. The specter of surveillance looms large as AI systems deployed in public and private spheres alike gain the capability to track, record, and infer details about an individual's life, habits, and preferences with alarming precision. Moreover, the risk extends beyond the mere data collection to encompass the potential for AI systems to derive sensitive information or make inferences that individuals might prefer to keep private, thus encroaching upon the sanctity of personal autonomy and anonymity.

Regulatory Considerations

The regulatory landscape governing data privacy in the age of AI is a patchwork of legislation, each striving to balance the scales between innovation and individual rights. Key among these regulations is the General Data Protection Regulation (GDPR) in the European Union. This pioneering legal framework sets stringent data collection, processing, and storage guidelines while empowering individuals with greater control over their personal information. Similarly, various jurisdictions worldwide have embarked on the journey to fortify their legal frameworks, introducing laws and guidelines specifically designed to address the unique challenges posed by AI. These regulations share a common goal: to ensure that as AI technologies evolve and permeate every corner of society, they do so within a framework that respects and protects privacy and data rights.

Best Practices for Data Protection

In navigating the precarious path between leveraging AI for its unparalleled potential and safeguarding against invasions of privacy, adherence to best practices in data protection emerges as a guiding principle. At the forefront of these practices is the principle of data minimization, a disciplined approach to data collection that advocates for acquiring only the information explicitly necessary for the task at hand. This is complemented by robust data anonymization techniques, which strip away personally identifiable information, rendering the data incapable of leading back to the individual it pertains to. Secure data storage further bolsters privacy protections, employing encryption and other security measures to shield personal information from unauthorized access or breaches. Additionally, implementing privacy by design, an approach that embeds privacy safeguards into the development process of AI systems from the outset, ensures that data protection is not an afterthought but an integral component of technological innovation.

Balancing Innovation and Privacy

The discourse on reconciling the dynamism of AI with the imperative of privacy protection unfolds across a broad spectrum of opinions and strategies. On one end, the argument posits that stringent privacy regulations might stifle innovation, placing undue constraints on the exploration and deployment of AI technologies. This perspective advocates for a regulatory environment that fosters innovation by allowing AI to flourish, albeit within a framework of accountability and oversight. Conversely, the counterargument emphasizes the paramount importance of privacy as a fundamental right that should not be compromised in pursuing technological advancement. This view champions robust privacy protections as the bedrock upon which trust in AI technologies can be built, arguing that innovation, to be sustainable and socially acceptable, must evolve within the boundaries of ethical and privacy-conscious practices.

Navigating this delicate balance demands a nuanced understanding of AI's transformative potential and privacy's intrinsic value. It requires a commitment to ongoing dialogue among technologists, policymakers, and the public, a conversation that explores the contours of what is technologically possible and what is ethically permissible. In this discourse, the pursuit of innovation becomes inextricably linked with respect for privacy, each informing and shaping the other in a continuous cycle of reflection, adjustment, and advancement.

FOSTERING TRANSPARENCY AND ACCOUNTABILITY IN AI DEPLOYMENTS

In the intricate weave of the digital age, where artificial intelligence (AI) threads through the fabric of daily life, the principles of transparency and accountability emerge as critical cornerstones. These principles act as ethical niceties and imperative mandates to instill trust and foster a sense of reliability in AI systems. The criticality of transparency in AI deployments cannot be overstated; it is the lighthouse guiding the ships of user trust and informed consent through the murky waters of complex algorithms and decision-making processes. Transparency, in essence, demystifies AI's workings, offering a clear view into the 'black box' that AI often represents, thereby empowering users with the understanding necessary to navigate AI-enhanced landscapes with confidence.

The quest for transparency in AI is multifaceted, embracing various methods designed to peel back the layers of complexity that cloak AI algorithms. One method gaining traction involves simplifying AI explanations, translating the dense fog of technical jargon into the clear light of day. This entails crafting explanations for AI decisions in a manner accessible to the layperson without sacrificing the depth of detail necessary for comprehensiveness. Another approach centers on the development of 'explainable AI' (XAI) systems, where the AI is designed from its inception to provide insight into its decision-making process, offering a window into the reasoning behind its conclusions. This proactive stance towards transparency ensures that AI systems are not just black boxes but open books, readable by those who interact with them.

Parallel to the pursuit of transparency runs the vein of accountability, a principle that ensures AI systems and their creators are answerable for the outcomes they produce. Accountability in AI is akin to the keystone in an arch, bearing the weight of ethical integrity and public trust. Mechanisms to uphold this principle span the spectrum from implementing audit trails to establishing oversight bodies. Audit trails serve as chronological records, tracing the decision-making path of AI systems and enabling the reconstruction and examination of decisions should concerns arise. Oversight bodies, on the other hand, act as guardians of ethical compliance, overseeing AI deployments to ensure they adhere to established ethical standards and regulations. These bodies, often composed of multidisciplinary experts, provide a balanced perspective, evaluating AI systems for their technical efficacy and adherence to ethical norms.

Yet, the path to achieving transparency and accountability in AI is fraught with challenges, each demanding innovative solutions. One such challenge lies in the inherent complexity of AI algorithms, which can make transparency a daunting task. The solution to this puzzle lies in the advancement of XAI technologies, focusing research and development efforts on creating AI systems that are inherently more interpretable. Additionally, the dynamic nature of AI, which learns and evolves, poses a challenge to maintaining consistent accountability. Addressing this requires establishing continuous monitoring systems capable of adapting to AI's evolution and ensuring ongoing compliance with ethical standards.

In the shadow of these challenges, the role of policy and regulation comes to the fore, acting as the scaffolding upon which efforts towards transparency and accountability are built. Legislation tailored to the nuances of AI can delineate clear guidelines for transparency and accountability, setting the stage for their incorporation into AI systems. Moreover, policies that encourage or mandate the disclosure of AI methodologies and impacts can further enhance transparency, making it a voluntary ethical choice and a compulsory requirement.

In this pursuit, the collaboration between AI developers, regulatory bodies, and the public becomes paramount. Developers must embrace the principles of transparency and accountability as foundational elements of AI design, embedding them into the DNA of AI systems. Armed with a deep understanding of AI's potential and pitfalls, regulatory bodies can craft policies that foster an environment where transparency and accountability are not just encouraged but expected. The public, informed about the workings and implications of AI, can exercise their voice and choice, advocating for systems that respect these principles.

Thus, the endeavor to weave transparency and accountability into the fabric of AI deployments is not a solitary journey but a collective effort. It requires the convergence of technical innovation, ethical consideration, and regulatory foresight, all directed toward creating AI systems that are not just intelligent but also comprehensible, reliable, and, above all, ethically sound. In this endeavor, transparency and accountability stand not as distant ideals but as attainable achievements, guiding the development and deployment of AI systems that enhance the world we live, not just with their capabilities but their integrity.

ETHICAL AI USE CASES: LESSONS FROM THE FIELD

In the intricate dance of innovation and ethics, artificial intelligence (AI) serves as a crucible where the calm waters of moral consideration temper the fires of creativity. This delicate balance is not mere philosophical rumination but a practical necessity, as evidenced by the myriad stories that unfold at the intersection of AI and ethical practice. These narratives, rich in their diversity, offer invaluable insights into how ethically conscious AI has sculpted landscapes of opportunity, rectified paths marred by oversight, and set standards for industries to aspire toward. Moreover, they cast light on the horizon, revealing the emerging ethical considerations accompanying AI technology's relentless march.

The positive impacts of ethically designed AI are manifold and profound, touching lives and transforming business landscapes. Consider the deployment of AI in enhancing accessibility for individuals with disabilities, a domain where ethical AI breaks down barriers and fosters inclusivity. In this context, AI-driven applications that translate sign language into text in real time stand as testaments to the potential of technology to serve humanity's highest ideals. Similarly, AI systems designed to monitor environmental health have empowered communities to advocate for cleaner, safer living conditions, showcasing how ethical considerations in AI development can extend their benefits beyond the digital realm into the very air we breathe and the water we drink.

Yet, the journey of integrating AI into the fabric of society is not without its missteps, each carrying lessons of pivotal importance. Instances where AI applications have faltered—be it through reinforcing existing biases in hiring practices or inadvertently compromising user privacy—serve as stark reminders of the vigilance required in ethical AI development. These cases highlight the critical need for diverse, inclusive teams in AI development processes, ensuring many perspectives are considered and potential pitfalls are identified and addressed long before they reach the end user. They underscore the importance of embedding ethical considerations at every stage of AI development, from conception through deployment, ensuring that the algorithms that increasingly influence our world do so in a manner that aligns with our collective values and aspirations.

Industries at the forefront of ethical AI use have set benchmarks that illuminate the path for others. The healthcare sector, for instance, has emerged as a field where the ethical use of AI is not just lauded but expected, with AI systems being deployed to predict patient outcomes, personalize treatment plans, and streamline operations while rigorously safeguarding patient confidentiality and autonomy. Similarly, the financial industry has begun navigating the ethical complexities of using AI for risk assessment and fraud detection, developing frameworks to ensure fair, transparent, and accountable decisions. These industry leaders demonstrate the feasibility of ethical AI use and its business imperative as trust and reliability become increasingly valuable currencies in the digital age.

Looking to the future, the evolution of AI technology presents new ethical considerations that demand our attention and foresight. For instance, the advent of autonomous decision-making systems raises questions about accountability in scenarios where human oversight is minimal. The potential for AI-driven personalization to morph into invasive surveillance underlines the need for robust privacy protections that evolve with technological capabilities. Moreover, the increasing integration of AI into critical infrastructure highlights the imperative for resilience against manipulation and sabotage, ensuring these systems can withstand technical failures and ethical breaches.

As we traverse this landscape, marked by the achievements of ethical AI use and the lessons drawn from its challenges, we gain insights and the resolve to continue pushing the boundaries of what technology can achieve when guided by a moral compass. The stories shared here serve as beacons, illuminating the way forward for AI development that is innovative, conscientious, powerful, and principled. They remind us that the true measure of our progress is not just in the sophistication of our technologies but in the depth of our commitment to using them wisely, responsibly, and ethically.

In closing, this exploration into the ethical dimensions of AI, from the uplifting tales of positive impact to the cautionary narratives of lessons learned, casts a spotlight on the essential role of ethics in the age of artificial intelligence. It underscores the need for continued vigilance, collaboration, and innovation to ensure that AI serves as a force for good, enhancing our capabilities without compromising our values. As we turn our gaze toward the future, let us carry forward the insights and aspirations gleaned from these stories, forging ahead into new territories of AI development with a steadfast commitment to ethical integrity at the core of all we do.

MITIGATING RISKS: SAFEGUARDING AI SYSTEMS

In the realm of artificial intelligence (AI), where innovation and adaptability reign supreme, the specter of security risks casts a long shadow, threatening to undermine the very foundations upon which these technological marvels are built. It's a scenario reminiscent of a bustling cityscape, where amid the architectural triumphs and neon-lit progress, the underbelly teems with vulnerabilities waiting to be exploited by those with nefarious intent. This chapter, crucial for the fortification of AI systems, is dedicated to casting a spotlight on these potential breaches, offering a blueprint for fortification that not only anticipates attacks but also weaves a robust defense into the fabric of AI's existence.

IDENTIFYING POTENTIAL AI SECURITY RISKS

Types of Security Risks

The landscape of AI security risks is as varied as it is daunting, with threats lurking in the digital ether and the tangible world. Among the most pervasive are data breaches, where sensitive information becomes the bounty for cyber pirates, and adversarial attacks, which see malicious actors manipulating AI systems to elicit unintended outcomes. Compounding these are risks of system hijacking, where control of AI functionalities is wrested away, and poisoning of the data well, wherein corrupted data skews AI learning, leading to flawed decisions.

Risk Assessment Tools

To navigate this minefield, a suite of practical risk assessment tools comes to the fore, acting as both a shield and a compass. Among these, AI vulnerability scanners scrutinize systems for weak spots, much like a diagnostic tool checks a car for faults before a journey. Equally vital are threat modeling methodologies that map out potential attack vectors, akin to a general charting of enemy routes before a battle. These tools, when wielded with precision, illuminate the path toward preemptive defense, ensuring that AI systems are not left to the mercy of chance or malice.

Vulnerabilities in AI Systems

The Achilles' heel of AI systems often lies in their complexity and the data that fuels them. Open-source AI models, for example, offer a double-edged sword; their accessibility fosters innovation but also leaves the door ajar for exploiters to study and subvert their mechanisms. Similarly, the reliance on vast datasets renders

AI susceptible to contamination, where even a single tainted datum can cascade into systemic errors, much like a drop of ink spreading in a glass of water.

Impact Analysis

The repercussions of security breaches in AI are not confined to the digital realm but ripple out, affecting businesses and consumers. Consider a scenario where a compromised AI system in a financial institution green-lights fraudulent transactions, leading to financial losses and eroded trust. Beyond immediate impacts, these breaches can tarnish reputations long-term, turning once-trusted names into bywords for vulnerability.

Visual Element: The Web of AI Security Risks

An infographic, "The Web of AI Security Risks," visually explores the multifaceted security threats facing AI systems. This web intricately details the types of risks, from data breaches spiraling out to adversarial attacks, and maps the pathways through which these risks can infiltrate AI systems. Accompanying this visual maze are pointers that guide the viewer on navigating these risks, akin to a guidebook for traversing a labyrinth, making the complex interconnections between different types of threats comprehensible at a glance.

In this dense landscape where technological prowess and security risks are in constant flux, the task of safeguarding AI systems emerges as a critical endeavor. It demands a proactive stance, one that anticipates threats, understands the vulnerabilities unique to AI, and is prepared to counteract these risks with a combination of sophisticated tools and strategic foresight. Your role as an IT professional, cybersecurity expert, or AI developer is crucial in this process. Your understanding of potential pitfalls and your ability to prevent them ensures that AI systems can continue to drive progress without falling prey to the shadows that loom over the digital horizon.

DEVELOPING A COMPREHENSIVE AI RISK MANAGEMENT PLAN

In the intricate ballet of artificial intelligence (AI) deployment, where each step and twirl must be meticulously choreographed to avoid missteps, crafting a strategic AI risk management plan emerges as the linchpin in maintaining poise and grace. Like a conductor's score, this plan orchestrates the myriad components of security, ensuring each is tuned to the overarching melody of safeguarding AI systems against the cacophony of risks that threaten to disrupt their harmony.

Components of a Risk Management Plan

A robust AI risk management plan comprises several critical components, each serving a specific role in the intricate dance of security. The cornerstone of this architectural marvel is risk identification, a process that meticulously catalogs potential threats, much like a cartographer mapping uncharted territories. Following closely is risk analysis, a detailed examination of the identified risks, assessing their nature and the possible havoc they might wreak, akin to a historian scrutinizing ancient texts to understand civilizations' rise and fall.

Central to this plan is risk evaluation, a reasonable process that weighs the severity of each risk against the likelihood of its occurrence, much like a jeweler assessing the value of gemstones. This evaluation informs the prioritization process, ensuring that resources are allocated efficiently, focusing first on the most menacing threats, reminiscent of a general strategizing the deployment of troops in anticipation of battle.

Integral to the plan's fabric are mitigation strategies, designed to either prevent risks from materializing or to minimize their impact should they breach the defenses. These strategies span a wide range, from technical safeguards like encryption and access controls to procedural measures such as staff training and incident response protocols. Embedded within this matrix is the importance of recovery strategies, detailing the steps to be taken in the aftermath of an incident to restore functionality and integrity to the AI systems, much like emergency protocols in place for urban centers facing natural disasters. This comprehensive plan should instill confidence in your ability to mitigate risks effectively.

Prioritizing Risks

The act of prioritizing risks within an AI system mirrors the meticulous curation of a museum exhibit, where artifacts are displayed not randomly but in a manner that guides the viewer through a narrative. This narrative is shaped by the potential impact of each risk and the probability of its occurrence. High-impact, high-probability risks demand immediate attention, much like a crack in a dam wall, whereas lower-impact, lower-probability risks may be monitored with less urgency, akin to preserving less critical but still valuable artifacts.

Mitigation Strategies

Mitigation strategies for AI systems are as diverse as the ecosystems within which these systems operate. One such strategy involves data encryption, a digital alchemy that transforms readable information into indecipherable code accessible only to those possessing the key. Another strategy is the implementation of access controls, akin to the guardians of a citadel, ensuring that only authorized personnel can interact with the AI systems, thereby reducing the risk of internal sabotage or data theft.

Regular software updates and patch management form another critical strategy akin to the upkeep of a city's infrastructure, ensuring that vulnerabilities are addressed before they can be exploited. Similarly, AI model resilience testing, through techniques like adversarial training, strengthens the system against manipulation attempts, much like fortifying a fortress against siege.

Plan Implementation and Monitoring

Implementing an AI risk management plan is not a one-off event but a dynamic process that evolves with the AI system it seeks to protect. This process begins with establishing a dedicated security team, akin to the appointment of sentinels, tasked with the ongoing vigilance required to detect and respond to threats. Regular training and drills ensure that all stakeholders are prepared to act swiftly and effectively in the event of a breach, much like a fire drill in a skyscraper.

Continuous monitoring is the thread that weaves through the risk management plan's fabric, ensuring that no stitch comes loose. This vigilance encompasses both the AI systems themselves and the broader cybersecurity landscape, alerting the sentinels to new threats on the horizon. Just as a ship's captain adjusts the sails to the changing wind, the risk management plan must also be flexible and ready to adapt to emerging threats and evolving technologies.

In the grand tapestry of AI deployment, developing and implementing a comprehensive risk management plan is a testament to the foresight and diligence required to navigate cybersecurity. Through meticulous planning, strategic prioritization, and dynamic adaptation, this plan ensures that AI systems remain functional and fortified against the diverse threats that undermine their integrity and efficacy.

CYBERSECURITY MEASURES FOR AI SYSTEMS

In the intricate web of our modern digital milieu, safeguarding artificial intelligence (AI) systems from malevolent forces necessitates a multifaceted strategy that is as dynamic and intelligent as the systems it seeks to protect. This segment illuminates the path forward, detailing methodologies for enhancing cybersecurity measures that underpin the robustness of AI systems, safeguard the sanctity of their data, and fortify the infrastructures within which they operate. Moreover, it underscores the pivotal role of human insight and vigilance through comprehensive training and awareness initiatives in creating a culture of security that acts as the first line of defense against cyber threats.

Cybersecurity Best Practices

Navigating the cybersecurity landscape requires a nuanced understanding that transcends conventional measures, adapting to the unique complexities introduced by AI technologies. Encryption emerges as a cornerstone, transforming data into a cryptic format indecipherable to unauthorized entities, ensuring that even in the event of a breach, the sanctity of the information remains uncompromised. Equally critical is implementing robust authentication protocols, demanding more than mere passwords to verify the identity of users accessing the system. This might include biometric verification or multi-factor authentication, creating layers of security that defy penetration.

Regular software audits and updates form the backbone of a proactive cybersecurity strategy. By identifying and rectifying vulnerabilities before they can be exploited, these audits act as a preemptive strike against potential breaches. Similarly, using secure coding practices to develop AI systems minimizes the risk of introducing exploitable flaws. This approach, akin to the meticulous craftsmanship of a master artisan, ensures that the very foundation upon which AI systems are built is impervious to attack.

Protecting AI Data

The lifeblood of AI systems is the data that fuels their learning and decision-making processes. Protecting this data requires a strategy that is both comprehensive and adaptable, capable of evolving in tandem with emerging threats. Data anonymization plays a crucial role in this endeavor, stripping away identifiable markers from datasets, thus rendering them useless to those with malicious intent. Moreover, the principle of least privilege ensures that access to sensitive data is strictly regulated and available only to those whose roles necessitate interaction with it. This systematic approach to access minimizes the risk of internal breaches, safeguarding against inadvertent leaks and deliberate sabotage.

The deployment of advanced monitoring systems offers real-time visibility into data transactions within AI systems, enabling the early detection of unusual patterns that may indicate a breach. These systems, vigilant sentinels of the digital domain, provide an additional layer of defense, ensuring that any attempt to compromise data integrity is swiftly identified and mitigated.

Securing AI Infrastructure

The infrastructure upon which AI systems rely, whether nestled within the confines of physical servers or diffused across the expanse of the cloud, demands rigorous security measures. Physical security measures, from surveillance cameras to biometric access controls, ensure that tangible assets are shielded from unauthorized access for on-premises environments. In contrast, cloud-based infrastructures benefit from the inherent security measures provided by cloud service providers, augmented by virtual private networks (VPNs) and firewalls that create a secure conduit for data transmission.

The segmentation of network infrastructure serves as a critical strategy, isolating different components of the AI system to contain potential breaches and prevent them from increasing across the network. While complex in its implementation, this compartmentalization strategy offers a means to minimize the impact of an attack, ensuring that the integrity of the broader system is preserved.

Training and Awareness

The human element within the cybersecurity ecosystem plays a pivotal role, acting as both a potential vulnerability and a critical asset. Comprehensive training and awareness programs are essential, equipping staff with the knowledge and skills to recognize and respond to cybersecurity threats. These programs should not be static but evolve, reflecting the changing nature of cyber threats and the continuing advancements in AI technology.

Simulated cyber-attack exercises, akin to drills conducted by emergency services, prepare staff for the eventuality of a breach, instilling the reflexes and instincts necessary to respond swiftly and effectively. Moreover, fostering a culture of security awareness ensures that cybersecurity is not viewed as the sole purview of IT departments but as a collective responsibility that permeates every level of the organization.

A multi-pronged strategy that encompasses technical measures, human insight, and organizational culture emerges as the blueprint for success in the quest to safeguard AI systems from the myriad threats that lurk within the digital shadows. This dynamic and adaptable strategy ensures that AI systems can continue to drive innovation and progress, shielded from the cyber threats that seek to undermine them.

DATA INTEGRITY AND PROTECTION IN AI OPERATIONS

The bedrock of artificial intelligence's (AI) prowess lies not merely in the sophistication of its algorithms or the computational power at its disposal but in the sanctity and reliability of the data that fuels its operations. In the grand tapestry of AI development, the thread of data integrity weaves through, binding disparate elements into a reliable, trustworthy, cohesive whole. This fidelity in data is paramount; it ensures that AI systems function as intended, make decisions, and generate insights that reflect reality accurately, untainted by corruption or manipulation. Within this context, the guardianship of data integrity becomes a task of utmost importance, a constant vigil to maintain the purity of the informational wellspring from which AI draws its strength.

Threats to the sanctity of this data emerge from various quarters, each with the potential to distort the lens through which AI views the world. Malicious interventions seek to poison this well, introducing flawed or biased data intending to skew AI operations towards erroneous outcomes. Natural entropy, too, plays its part, as degradation in data quality over time—a consequence of neglect or inadequate maintenance—can lead to a gradual erosion of system reliability. Even the inadvertent introduction of errors during data collection and processing stages poses significant risks, turning the data stream into a potential source of falsehood rather than a beacon of truth.

A multifaceted shield is deployed to counteract these threats, a set of mechanisms designed to preserve data integrity across the AI lifecycle. Foremost among these is the implementation of rigorous data validation protocols, a procedural checkpoint that scrutinizes incoming data for accuracy and relevance, much like a vigilant gatekeeper ensuring that only the worthy pass. Encryption is another bulwark, a cryptographic veil that protects data from prying eyes, ensuring its sanctity is preserved even in the face of attempted breaches. Furthermore, redundancy, the strategic duplication of data across multiple storage sites, safeguards against loss, ensuring that even in the event of a catastrophic failure, the informational core of AI operations remains intact.

Beyond these technical measures, the role of compliance and governance frameworks comes to the fore, providing a structured canopy under which data integrity and protection efforts flourish. These frameworks, born of regulatory wisdom and ethical considerations, establish the standards to which AI operations must adhere, defining the boundaries of acceptable practice. They mandate regular audits, ensuring that adherence to data protection standards is not merely aspirational but a documented reality. Through compliance certifications, they offer a seal of approval, a mark of trust that signals to stakeholders the system's commitment to upholding data integrity.

These governance frameworks are not static edicts carved in stone but living documents that evolve in response to the shifting landscape of technology and societal norms. They incorporate feedback loops, allowing for integrating lessons learned from operational experiences and technological advancements. This adaptability ensures that the frameworks remain relevant, guiding AI operations through the uncertain terrain of future developments with a steady hand.

Maintaining its integrity can be balanced in the crucible of AI development, where data is the raw material and the fuel that drives innovation. This task demands constant vigilance, a commitment to best practices, and an adherence to ethical and regulatory standards. Through these efforts, AI systems are fortified against the myriad threats that loom, ensuring that their operations are reliable and worthy of their trust.

BUILDING RESILIENCE: PREPARING FOR AI-RELATED CONTINGENCIES

In the dynamic realm of artificial intelligence (AI), where innovation's pace seldom wanes, resilience against unforeseen risks and contingencies emerges as a linchpin for sustained operational integrity. This resilience, akin to the adaptability of a seasoned navigator charting through tumultuous seas, ensures that AI systems remain robust in the face of adversities, be they security breaches, data integrity lapses, or unforeseen operational failures. This resilience enables organizations to maintain continuity, safeguard stakeholders' interests, and uphold the trust invested in technological advancements.

Developing a Resilience Strategy

Crafting a resilience strategy for AI-related risks commences with a meticulous assessment of the ecosystem within which these systems operate, identifying the potential points of failure and the ripple effects such failures might engender across interconnected operations. This strategy demands an inherently flexible architecture, allowing for rapid reconfiguration in response to emerging threats and vulnerabilities. It necessitates establishing redundant systems distributed across diverse infrastructures, ensuring that the compromise of a singular node does not precipitate a systemic collapse. Furthermore, an emphasis on modular design facilitates the isolation and rectification of issues without necessitating a complete system overhaul, thereby minimizing downtime and preserving operational continuity.

Incident Response Planning

Formulating an incident response plan tailored to AI-related security incidents involves orchestrating a multidisciplinary team, unified by a singular mandate—to swiftly and effectively address and neutralize threats. This team operates under a well-defined protocol, delineating clear roles and responsibilities, ensuring that the response is immediate and efficacious when an incident arises. Central to this plan is the establishment of communication channels, both internal and external, enabling the dissemination of timely and accurate information to relevant stakeholders, thereby mitigating the cascading effects of misinformation and panic. Simulation exercises mirror a spectrum of potential incidents, hone the team's reflexes, and ingrain procedural muscle memory that ensures a coordinated and composed response under pressure.

Recovery and Restoration

The aftermath of an AI-related security breach necessitates a deliberate approach to recovery and restoration, transcending mere technical rectification to address the broader implications of the incident. This process begins with a thorough investigation, uncovering the breach's root cause and implementing corrective measures to fortify vulnerabilities and prevent recurrence. Equally critical is the restoration of operations, a phased approach that prioritizes critical functions to swiftly resume service delivery, thereby minimizing the impact on stakeholders. This phase also involves a transparent and candid dialogue with affected parties, acknowledging the breach's ramifications and outlining the measures to address them, restoring confidence in the organization's commitment to security and operational integrity.

Learning and Adapting

The true measure of resilience lies not in an organization's capacity to withstand adversity but in its ability to learn from these experiences, adapting its strategies to fortify against future occurrences. This learning process entails a rigorous post-incident analysis, distilling actionable insights from the breach and integrating these learnings into the organization's operational DNA. It demands a culture that views failures not as points of finality but as springboards for growth, fostering an environment where continuous improvement is encouraged and ingrained. Through this cycle of learning and adaptation, organizations evolve, transforming potential vulnerabilities into bastions of strength, thereby ensuring that with each challenge surmounted, the resilience of their AI systems is further augmented.

In navigating the complex and ever-evolving landscape of artificial intelligence, building resilience against AI-related risks and contingencies is a testament to an organization's foresight, adaptability, and commitment to excellence. It underscores an acknowledgment that vigilance and preparedness are indispensable allies in pursuing technological advancement. As we advance to the subsequent chapters, this foundation of resilience informs our exploration of AI's boundless possibilities. It ensures that these forays into the unknown are anchored in a commitment to security, integrity, and the unwavering pursuit of progress.

STAYING AHEAD: NAVIGATING THE AI REVOLUTION

Against the backdrop of a rapidly evolving digital landscape, the imperative for business leaders to remain at the forefront of artificial intelligence (AI) advancements has never been more pronounced. This urgency is not born of a mere desire to keep pace but from the recognition that the mastery of AI trends and developments is a critical determinant in sculpting the future of industries. It's akin to the way a surfer must read, anticipate, and position themselves for the wave long before it breaks; missing the cue does not just mean missing the wave - it risks being overtaken by it. As business leaders, you have the power to shape this wave and steer your industries toward a future driven by AI innovation.

TRACKING AI TRENDS: RESOURCES AND TOOLS FOR LEADERS

Leveraging Industry Insights

For leaders aiming to harness AI's full potential, integrating industry insights is a practical and effective strategy. This involves a diligent perusal of industry reports, AI newsletters, and thought leadership articles, which collectively serve as a compass guiding through the terrain of AI advancements. By setting aside dedicated time weekly to digest a curated list of publications from reputable sources such as AI research institutes, leading technology firms, and academic journals, leaders can ensure a broad and informed perspective. This fosters an environment where strategic decisions are underpinned by a deep understanding of AI's trajectory and ensures that leaders are well-equipped to navigate the AI revolution.

Utilizing AI Analytics Tools

In an era where data reigns supreme, AI analytics tools emerge as indispensable allies for leaders. These tools, sophisticated in their ability to sift through and analyze vast datasets, offer real-time insights into AI advancements, performance metrics, and competitive analysis. Imagine integrating these tools into the daily workflow, transforming raw data into actionable intelligence that informs product development, marketing strategies, and operational efficiencies. For instance, employing an AI analytics platform that tracks user engagement and behavior can unveil patterns and preferences, enabling a tailored approach that resonates with the target audience.

Participating in AI Communities

Active participation in online forums, social media groups, and professional networks dedicated to AI is not just a way to stay updated but a strategic move for business leaders. This engagement is not a passive activity but an active dialogue where challenges are shared, solutions are brainstormed, and new technologies are debated. It's like attending a global symposium from one's desk, where the collective wisdom of the AI community serves to elevate knowledge and spur innovation. By encouraging their teams to join relevant AI communities, share their insights, and bring back learnings, leaders can drive internal innovation and growth and ensure that their organizations are at the forefront of AI advancements.

Continuous Learning Culture

The essence of keeping pace with AI advancements lies not solely in the acquisition of knowledge but in cultivating a culture that champions continuous learning. This culture, nurtured within the organization, encourages curiosity, experimentation, and the relentless pursuit of excellence. It involves not just the top echelons of leadership but permeates every tier, empowering individuals with the tools, resources, and opportunities to expand their AI acumen. Workshops, seminars, and online courses become staples, while internal knowledge-sharing sessions and innovation labs become the crucibles where theory meets practice. This learning culture ensures that the organization does not merely react to AI advancements but anticipates and shapes them. Embrace this culture of continuous learning, and you will find yourself at the forefront of AI innovation.

Visual Element: AI Trend Tracker Dashboard

To bring these concepts to life, consider the implementation of an "AI Trend Tracker Dashboard." This interactive tool, accessible to all team members, aggregates real-time data on AI trends, industry reports, and analytics insights. It features customizable widgets that allow users to tailor the dashboard to their specific interests and responsibilities, whether the latest in machine learning algorithms, AI applications in marketing, or breakthroughs in natural language processing. The dashboard also incorporates a "Learning Hub" where employees can access recommended reading materials, sign up for upcoming workshops, and participate in discussion forums. This tool centralizes AI knowledge and resources and serves as a tangible manifestation of the organization's commitment to fostering a culture of continuous learning and innovation in AI.

Navigating the AI revolution demands more than passive observation; it requires active engagement, strategic foresight, and an unwavering commitment to continuous improvement. By leveraging industry insights, utilizing analytics tools, participating in AI communities, and fostering a culture of continuous learning, leaders can ensure their organizations not only stay ahead of the curve but also shape the trajectory of AI's impact on their industries. But remember, you are not alone in this journey. Strategic partnerships with AI entities can accelerate your progress, aligning your goals and resources towards AI-driven innovation. Together, we can shape the future of industries.

INNOVATING WITH AI: FOSTERING A CULTURE OF CONTINUOUS IMPROVEMENT

In artificial intelligence (AI), the static landscapes of yesteryears are fast giving way to dynamic ecosystems, pulsating with the rhythms of innovation and transformation. Within this context, cultivating a milieu that accommodates and actively promotes experimentation with AI technologies forms the bedrock upon which organizations can sculpt their future. This commitment to exploration, safeguarded by parameters that ensure risks are calculated and contained, ignites creativity, urging teams to push beyond the conventional boundaries of possibility.

Strategies to foster this environment of experimentation are manifold, each tailored to align with an organization's unique ethos and objectives. Initiating hackathons, for instance, emerges as a potent catalyst, propelling individuals and teams toward developing novel AI solutions within the crucible of competition and camaraderie. These events, often marked by a frenetic pace of ideation and prototyping, serve as incubators for groundbreaking ideas and platforms for cross-pollination across departments and disciplines. Similarly, instituting an innovation sandbox offers a digital playground where ideas can be tested, iterated, and refined without the overhang of operational disruptions. Like a laboratory, this sandbox becomes a space where failure is not a setback but a stepping stone towards refinement and success.

The iterative approach to AI projects, championed as a cornerstone of agile methodologies, further underscores the philosophy of continuous improvement. This approach, characterized by its cyclical nature of planning, implementing, testing, and reviewing, ensures that AI projects are not monolithic undertakings but fluid and adaptable ventures. Each iteration becomes an opportunity to refine and enhance, drawing on insights from real-world applications and user feedback. This cycle, relentlessly pursuing excellence, ensures that AI solutions remain relevant and at the cutting edge of technological advancement.

Leveraging AI for process optimization within internal operations reveals another dimension of innovation, where the focus shifts from external offerings to internal efficiencies. Here, AI becomes a tool not for creating new products but for reimagining existing processes, streamlining operations, and unlocking efficiencies previously obscured by the limitations of human oversight. An AI-driven approach to inventory management, for instance, can predict fluctuations in demand with a precision that eludes even the most experienced professionals, ensuring that supply chains are resilient and responsive. Similarly, AI-enhanced recruitment processes can sift through vast pools of candidates, identifying ideal matches based on criteria that extend beyond the superficial, thereby enriching the talent pool with individuals whose potential might have been overlooked.

The narrative of continuous AI innovation is punctuated by success stories from organizations that have embraced this ethos, transforming their operations and, by extension, their industries. A case in point is a tech giant that revolutionized customer service by deploying AI-driven virtual assistants. These assistants, capable of understanding and responding to customer queries with empathy and precision previously unattainable, not only elevated the customer experience but also set a new benchmark for the industry. Another illustration is a logistics company that employed AI to optimize its delivery routes, reducing fuel consumption and improving delivery times—an initiative that bolstered its bottom line and contributed to environmental sustainability.

These stories, each a testament to the transformative power of AI, underscore the impact of fostering a culture of continuous improvement. They highlight how organizations, by encouraging experimentation, adopting an iterative approach, leveraging AI for internal optimization, and drawing inspiration from success stories, can not only navigate the complexities of the AI revolution but also emerge as architects of this new digital frontier.

AI AND THE FUTURE OF WORK: PREPARING YOUR WORKFORCE

In an era when artificial intelligence (AI) reshapes industry contours, equipping the workforce with a repertoire of future-oriented skills emerges as a strategic imperative. This task, intricate in its demands, requires a nuanced understanding of the symbiosis between human creativity and machine intelligence. The skills pivotal in this AI-driven future transcend technical prowess, embracing adaptability, critical thinking, and the ability to interact seamlessly with increasingly intelligent systems.

Cultivating these capabilities within the workforce necessitates a multifaceted approach, where traditional learning paradigms are augmented by innovative pedagogies that mirror the dynamism of AI itself. Initiatives aimed at reskilling and upskilling employees must thus be as agile and forward-thinking as the technologies they seek to master. The objective is two-fold: to forge a workforce that is proficient in leveraging AI for operational excellence and adept at navigating the ethical and societal implications of these powerful tools.

In talent management, AI's predictive capabilities offer transformative potential. By analyzing vast datasets on career progression, skill acquisition, and job performance, AI can unveil patterns and trends that inform strategic workforce planning. This foresight allows organizations to anticipate future skill requirements, identify burgeoning talent gaps, and implement targeted development programs. The result is a talent management strategy that is proactive and precision-tuned to the evolving work landscape.

Developing comprehensive learning programs and resources underpins creating an AI-savvy workforce. These educational frameworks, designed with an eye towards inclusivity and accessibility, aim to democratize AI knowledge across all levels of the organization. From immersive workshops that simulate real-world AI applications to online courses that offer flexibility and breadth, the goal is to foster an environment where continuous learning is encouraged and ingrained in the organizational culture.

Embedding such a culture requires a recalibration of traditional learning metrics, where the emphasis shifts from completing training modules to applying acquired knowledge in innovative and impactful ways. It also calls for reassessing the learning tools at our disposal and integrating AI into the educational process. AI-driven platforms can personalize learning experiences, adapting content and pacing to meet the individual needs of each employee. This personalization enhances learning outcomes and reflects the broader trend of customization that AI brings to various aspects of organizational life.

Moreover, the journey towards an AI-empowered workforce is iterative, characterized by continuous feedback loops between employees and AI systems. This interaction fosters a symbiotic relationship where both humans and machines learn from each other, enhancing the former's capabilities while refining the latter's algorithms. It is a dynamic process that underscores the transformative impact of AI on the workforce, not as a tool of displacement but as a catalyst for growth and innovation.

To anchor these initiatives in practicality, organizations can look towards implementing AI in talent management as both a model and a method. By leveraging AI to predict future workforce needs, businesses can rapidly tailor their reskilling and upskilling programs. This application of AI exemplifies its potential to enhance operational efficiency and serves as a blueprint for its role in nurturing human capital.

However, creating such an AI-savvy workforce extends beyond the confines of organizational boundaries. It necessitates a collaborative effort that spans industries, academia, and governmental bodies. Partnerships with educational institutions can provide employees access to cutting-edge research and thought leadership in AI. At the same time, collaboration with regulatory agencies ensures that workforce development programs remain aligned with emerging legal and ethical standards.

This collective endeavor, marked by a shared commitment to harnessing the potential of AI, paves the way for a future where work is not defined by the limitations of human or machine alone but by the synergies between them. It envisions a workforce that is not just equipped to use AI but inspired to push the boundaries of what it can achieve. In this future, the skills of critical thinking, ethical reasoning, and collaborative innovation stand as the hallmarks of success, ensuring that as we stride forward into the

AI-augmented horizon, we do so with a workforce as resilient as it is visionary.

STRATEGIC PARTNERSHIPS: COLLABORATING FOR AI SUCCESS

In the intricate mosaic of the AI landscape, the strategic alliances formed between businesses and technology purveyors or academic entities stand as a testament to the axiom that unity fosters strength. This collaboration, far from a mere confluence of resources, evolves into a symbiotic relationship where shared visions and complementary capabilities accelerate the journey toward AI-driven innovation. In this context, discerning the criteria for selecting the right partners becomes pivotal, ensuring that these alliances are not just marriages of convenience but unions rooted in shared objectives and mutual respect.

Choosing the Right AI Partners

The selection of technology partners, akin to the cultivation of rare and delicate orchids, demands meticulous attention to the compatibility of goals, values, and visions for the future. This harmony is not superficial but extends to the core of what each entity represents. A potential partner's track record in innovation, commitment to ethical AI practices, and the robustness of their technology portfolio emerge as critical indicators of their suitability. Furthermore, the flexibility and scalability of their solutions offer insights into how well they can adapt to evolving needs, ensuring that the partnership remains relevant in the face of rapidly changing market dynamics. This alignment, when achieved, sets the stage for a collaboration that transcends transactional interactions, fostering a relationship where shared success becomes the ultimate objective.

Collaboration Models

The tapestry of collaboration between businesses and AI entities is woven with various threads, each representing a model distinct in its structure yet unified in its purpose. At one end of the spectrum lies the joint venture, a model epitomized by shared investments in AI projects that aim to blend the technological prowess of AI firms with the market insights and operational expertise of established businesses. This model thrives on mutual stakes in success, driving a deep-seated commitment to realizing shared goals.

On another front, research partnerships with academic institutions illuminate the path toward cutting-edge AI advancements. These alliances, often underpinned by access to unparalleled research capabilities and fresh perspectives from the academic world, serve as crucibles for innovation that might need to be more speculative or long-term for commercial entities to pursue independently. Here, exchanging knowledge, resources, and experimental freedom paves the way for breakthroughs that can redefine industries.

Co-Innovation with Partners

The essence of co-innovation lies in the amalgamation of distinct capabilities, knowledge bases, and perspectives, culminating in creating AI solutions that are novel and deeply integrated into the fabric of business operations. This process, characterized by iterative ideation, prototyping, and refinement cycles, benefits immensely from the diversity of strategic partnerships. Co-innovation projects often see teams navigating uncharted territories, leveraging AI to address complex challenges that defy conventional solutions. The logistical framework for such endeavors hinges on clear communication channels, defined roles, and shared platforms where ideas can germinate, evolve, and come to fruition. The benefits, ranging from accelerated innovation cycles to access to niche expertise, underscore the transformative potential of collaborative endeavors in AI.

Case Studies of Successful AI Partnerships

The landscape of AI is dotted with stories of successful partnerships that have not only accelerated AI initiatives but also set new benchmarks for what collaboration can achieve. One such narrative unfolds in healthcare, where a tech company's alliance with a network of hospitals led to the development of an AI-driven diagnostic tool. This tool, capable of analyzing medical images with unprecedented accuracy, was the product of combining the tech company's AI algorithms with the hospital network's vast repository of medical data and clinical expertise. The result was a solution that enhanced diagnostic accuracy and significantly reduced the time required for identifying critical conditions, thereby saving lives.

Another illustrative example is found in the retail sector, where a partnership between a retail giant and an AI startup revolutionized inventory management. The startup's innovative AI platform, tailored through collaboration to align with the retailer's operational nuances, offered predictive insights into inventory needs with a previously unattainable precision level. This partnership optimized stock levels across hundreds of stores and paved the way for a more dynamic and responsive supply chain, reducing waste and enhancing customer satisfaction.

These case studies, each a mosaic piece in the larger picture of AI's impact, highlight the profound influence that strategic partnerships can wield in AI. Through the fusion of diverse expertise, shared visions, and a commitment to co-innovation, these alliances illuminate the path toward a future where AI's potential is realized and magnified, driving progress that transcends the sum of its parts.

THE NEXT FRONTIER: EXPLORING CUTTING-EDGE AI TECHNOLOGIES

In the vast expanse of the artificial intelligence (AI) landscape, a constellation of emerging technologies beckons with promise, each harboring the potential to redefine paradigms across industries. The horizon is ablaze with innovations like quantum computing's entanglement with AI, offering computational abilities that dwarf today's standards, or the nuanced complexities of affective computing, poised to endow machines with the subtleties of human emotion recognition. While still in their nascent stages, these technologies signal a shift towards an era where AI's capabilities are not just enhanced but fundamentally transformed.

Navigating this terrain, where the future of AI unfolds in real time, demands a framework that balances the allure of innovation with the pragmatism of business viability. This assessment begins with a meticulous analysis of the technology's readiness, probing its current state and the trajectory of its evolution. The inquiry extends to its integration within existing systems and processes, evaluating whether it complements or disrupts the established order. Moreover, the examination of potential impacts, both direct and indirect, on the business's value chain becomes crucial, offering insights into how these technologies might reshape market positions, customer experiences, and competitive landscapes.

Investing in cutting-edge AI technologies becomes an exercise in balancing the scales of risk and reward. On the one hand, the allure of first-mover advantages tempts with promises of market dominance and brand differentiation. Conversely, the specter of untested technologies and uncertain returns urges caution. This delicate balance hinges not just on financial considerations but also on an organization's appetite for innovation, its capacity to absorb and adapt to new technologies, and the resilience of its operational backbone to withstand potential upheavals.

In this context, future-proofing an organization's AI strategy is critical. This process, far from a defensive stance against obsolescence, is an active engagement with the fluidity of technological advancement. It involves fostering a culture of agility where strategies are not cast in stone but remain open to adaptation as new information and technologies surface. It also necessitates the cultivation of a versatile talent pool equipped with the skills of today and the learning agility to navigate tomorrow's landscapes. Moreover, modular technology architectures ensure systems can evolve incrementally, integrating new capabilities without necessitating wholesale transformations.

Therefore, the exploration of cutting-edge AI technologies is not a solitary voyage into the unknown but a collective journey that intertwines the destinies of businesses, technologies, and societies. It's a journey punctuated by moments of discovery, where the potential of AI to drive sustainable growth, enhance human experiences, and solve complex global challenges comes into sharper focus. It's a narrative of progress, marked by the convergence of human ingenuity and machine intelligence, where the boundaries of what's possible are continually expanded.

As this chapter draws to a close, the exploration of emerging AI technologies stands not just as a testament to human curiosity and ambition but as a beacon for future endeavors. The framework for assessing new technologies, balanced investments, and future-proofing strategies delineate a path that acknowledges the complexity of innovation while embracing the opportunities it presents. In this narrative, the emergence of cutting-edge AI technologies is not an endpoint but a waypoint, marking progress in the ongoing journey of AI evolution. The broader vista that unfolds is one of continuous adaptation, where the relentless pursuit of innovation ensures that businesses survive and thrive in tomorrow's landscapes. As we transition towards the next chapter, this exploration serves as a foundation, informing and inspiring the strategies and decisions that will shape the future of AI in business.

STEERING BUSINESSES THROUGH THE AI REVOLUTION

In a time where the tapestry of business is continuously interwoven with threads of technological advancements, the imperative for leaders to not only recognize but also adeptly navigate the domain of artificial intelligence (AI) becomes paramount. The signposts of this era are not etched in the familiar landmarks of the past. Still, they are illuminated by the beacon of AI, guiding businesses toward uncharted territories teeming with potential. This chapter delves into the quintessential role of visionary leadership in steering organizations through the transformative seas of AI, emphasizing the critical importance of adopting a visionary mindset, crafting a compelling AI vision, navigating the evolving AI landscape, and inspiring organization-wide enthusiasm for AI adoption.

ADOPTING A VISIONARY MINDSET

Adopting a visionary mindset transcends conventional strategic thinking in the realm of AI, where possibilities stretch beyond the horizon. It's akin to an architect envisioning a structure that harmonizes with its surroundings and stands as a testament to innovation. Leaders must cultivate a mindset that perceives AI not as a mere tool but as a transformative force capable of reshaping the fabric of their business operations, creating value that permeates every facet of the organization.

A Real-life Example: Implementing AI in Customer Service

Consider a scenario where a retail company, recognizing its customers' burgeoning expectations for seamless and personalized experiences, decides to implement AI-powered chatbots. The decision, rooted in a visionary mindset, aims to enhance customer service efficiency and redefine the customer journey, making each interaction a stepping stone toward loyalty and satisfaction. The leader, in this case, sees beyond the immediate benefits, envisioning a future where AI becomes a cornerstone of customer relationship management, crafting experiences that are not only responsive but also anticipatory.

Setting an AI Vision

The cornerstone of navigating the AI era is the articulation of a clear, compelling AI vision that serves as the organization's North Star. This vision encapsulates the aspirations and objectives of integrating AI into business operations and delineates the path towards achieving them. It's a beacon that guides the strategic alignment of AI initiatives with the overarching business goals, ensuring that every technological endeavor is a step towards realizing the envisioned future.

Visual Element: The AI Vision Blueprint

A visual representation, "The AI Vision Blueprint," offers leaders a structured framework for developing their AI vision. This blueprint, presented as an infographic, outlines key components such as defining the purpose of AI integration, identifying the areas of impact, setting measurable objectives, and aligning with long-term business goals. It serves as a visual guide that simplifies the vision creation process, ensuring leaders can effectively communicate their AI aspirations to organizational stakeholders.

Navigating the AI Landscape

The landscape of AI is dynamic, marked by rapid advancements and shifting paradigms. Leaders must keep abreast of these changes and possess the acumen to discern which trends are relevant to their business. This navigation involves strategically evaluating AI technologies, assessing their potential to drive innovation, optimize operations, or unlock new market opportunities. It's a process akin to a navigator charting a course through shifting seas, where the ability to adapt and recalibrate based on new information is crucial for reaching the desired destination.

The Role of Strategic AI Investments

A critical aspect of navigating the AI landscape is making strategic decisions about AI investments. This entails a thorough analysis of the potential ROI of AI projects, considering factors such as cost, implementation complexity, and alignment with business objectives. Leaders must weigh these considerations, balancing the pursuit of innovation with financial prudence to ensure that AI initiatives drive sustainable growth.

Inspiring AI Adoption

The successful integration of AI into business operations hinges on the organization-wide enthusiasm and acceptance of these technologies. Leaders play a pivotal role in inspiring this adoption, acting as champions of change who can articulate the value of AI in compelling narratives that resonate across the organization. This inspiration is not a one-time endeavor but a continuous effort that involves showcasing successes, addressing concerns, and fostering an environment where experimentation and learning from failures are encouraged.

Interactive Element: AI Adoption Challenge

An engaging exercise, "The AI Adoption Challenge," invites team members to ideate and submit proposals for AI projects that could solve existing business challenges or unlock new opportunities. This interactive challenge stimulates creativity and involvement and serves as a platform for leaders to identify and nurture AI advocates within the organization, furthering the cause of AI adoption.

In steering businesses through the AI revolution, leaders are called upon to embody the qualities of visionaries, architects, navigators, and champions. Adopting a visionary mindset, crafting a clear AI vision, strategically navigating the AI landscape, and inspiring organization-wide enthusiasm for AI adoption form the pillars upon which businesses can thrive in this era of technological transformation.

BUILDING AI LITERACY ACROSS YOUR ORGANIZATION

In the fluid tapestry of today's corporate ecosystems, the proliferation of artificial intelligence (AI) stands as both a harbinger of transformative potential and a clarion call for a seismic shift in organizational skill sets. To traverse this evolving landscape, the cultivation of AI literacy across the breadth and depth of an organization not only serves as a strategic imperative but also a cornerstone for fostering an environment where innovation and adaptability flourish. This necessitates a multifaceted approach, weaving together education, training, mentorship, and evaluation into a coherent strategy that elevates AI understanding from the executive suite to the operational core.

The initiation of AI education programs marks the first stride towards demystifying AI for the collective workforce, addressing the diverse roles and knowledge levels that populate the organization. This endeavor, far from a monolithic exercise, requires a nuanced understanding of the distinct learning needs that vary by department, role, and individual proficiency. Tailoring educational content that spans the gamut from foundational principles of AI to advanced applications in specific business functions ensures that each organization member finds relevance and value in the learning journey. For instance, sales teams might delve into AI's role in predictive analytics for customer behavior, while product development units explore machine learning models for enhancing product features. This tailored approach facilitates deeper engagement and ensures that AI education translates into practical value, embedding AI's potential into the fabric of daily operations.

Simultaneously, the leverage of AI within training programs emerges as a meta-layer of innovation, showcasing the capabilities these initiatives aim to elucidate. AI-driven training platforms, equipped with adaptive learning algorithms, offer personalized learning experiences that adjust to the learner's pace and understanding in real-time. This personalization ensures that each employee's educational journey is efficient and effective, maximizing knowledge retention and application. Furthermore, these platforms can generate insights into learning patterns, identifying areas where additional focus is necessary and allowing for the iterative refinement of training content. The result is a dynamic, self-optimizing training ecosystem that educates and embodies the principles of AI it seeks to impart.

Central to the propagation of AI literacy is the cultivation of AI champions within the organization. These individuals, selected for their proficiency in and passion for AI, serve as mentors and advocates, accelerating the diffusion of AI knowledge across the organization. Their role transcends the mere dissemination of information, encompassing the inspiration of colleagues, the facilitation of hands-on workshops, and the guidance of teams in the practical application of AI in their respective domains. AI champions act as the connective tissue between the abstract potential of AI and its tangible impact on business outcomes, embodying the bridge from knowledge to action. Their presence fosters a culture of curiosity and experimentation, crucial ingredients for innovation in the AI domain.

Measuring improvements in AI literacy across the organization introduces a quantifiable dimension to the educational endeavor, offering a lens through which progress can be assessed and strategies recalibrated. This evaluation, however, extends beyond traditional metrics of course completion or test scores, venturing into the assessment of practical application and impact. Metrics such as the increase in AI-driven projects, enhancements in efficiency attributed to AI applications, and the frequency of AI discussions in strategic meetings serve as barometers for the depth and breadth of AI literacy. Additionally, feedback mechanisms, incorporating surveys and interviews, provide qualitative insights into the effectiveness of training programs and the perceived value of AI in enhancing job performance. This holistic approach to evaluation ensures that AI literacy initiatives remain aligned with organizational objectives, driving continuous improvement in content and delivery.

In the intricate dance of integrating AI into the fabric of an organization, the strategy for building AI literacy unfolds as a nuanced ballet of education, application, and evaluation. It is a strategy that recognizes the multifaceted nature of AI, its implications for various roles within the organization, and the imperative for a workforce that is not only conversant in AI terminology but also proficient in leveraging its capabilities. Organizations can navigate the complexities of the AI revolution through tailored educational programs, the innovative use of AI in training, the cultivation of AI champions, and the meticulous measurement of literacy improvements. This journey, marked by continuous learning and adaptation, ensures that businesses remain agile and innovative, poised to capitalize on the transformative potential of AI.

CULTIVATING ETHICAL LEADERSHIP FOR AI INITIATIVES

In the intricate web of technological advancement, where artificial intelligence (AI) stands as a beacon of progress, the moral compass guiding its integration into the corporate sphere is paramount. The creation and enforcement of ethical frameworks within organizations are not merely acts of compliance but foundational elements that ensure AI initiatives enhance societal well-being while mitigating risks of harm. In this context, the mantle of ethical leadership assumes a critical role, embodying the principles that navigate the complex interplay between innovation and responsibility.

Ethical Frameworks for AI

The bedrock of responsible AI use within any organization is establishing a robust ethical framework. This foundational document, akin to a constitution, delineates the core values, principles, and standards governing AI technologies' development, deployment, and utilization. Such a framework requires a multidisciplinary approach, engaging stakeholders across various domains—from legal experts and technologists to ethicists and end-users. This collective effort ensures that the framework addresses a comprehensive spectrum of ethical concerns, from data privacy and bias mitigation to transparency and accountability. Moreover, the dynamic nature of AI technology and its societal implications necessitates that these frameworks are living documents, subject to regular review and revision in response to emerging challenges and insights.

Implementing these ethical frameworks involves embedding their principles into every phase of the AI project lifecycle. This integration begins at the conceptualization stage, where ethical considerations influence project scope and objectives and extends through development, deployment, and beyond, ensuring ongoing compliance and ethical alignment. Furthermore, operationalizing these frameworks relies on developing practical tools and methodologies—such as ethical AI checklists, impact assessments, and audit mechanisms—that facilitate their application in day-to-day activities, transforming abstract principles into actionable practices.

Role of Leaders in Ethical AI

Leaders within organizations wield considerable influence in setting the tone for ethical AI practices. Their commitment to ethical standards and decision-making processes serves as a model for the organization, cultivating a culture where ethical considerations are integral to AI initiatives. Leaders demonstrate this commitment through clear communication of ethical expectations, allocating resources to support ethical AI practices, and establishing accountability structures that ensure these practices are upheld. Moreover, by championing transparency in AI operations, leaders foster trust among stakeholders, reinforcing the organization's reputation as a responsible innovator in AI.

Leaders must proactively engage in ethical deliberations and decision-making processes related to AI. This involvement ensures that ethical considerations receive the attention they deserve at the highest levels of decision-making but also encourages a participatory approach to ethical governance. Leaders promote a collaborative environment where ethical dilemmas are addressed with collective wisdom and insight by soliciting input from diverse stakeholders and fostering open dialogues on ethical challenges.

Addressing Ethical Dilemmas

Ethical dilemmas in developing and deploying AI technologies are inevitable, given the complex interdependencies between technological capabilities, business objectives, and societal impacts. Strategies for addressing these dilemmas involve:

- A nuanced understanding of the ethical principles at stake.
- A rigorous analysis of potential outcomes.
- A commitment to finding solutions that align with the organization's ethical framework.

Decision-making in these contexts benefits from structured processes, such as ethical decision trees or matrices, which guide stakeholders through a systematic evaluation of options, considering factors such as the potential for harm, the distribution of benefits and burdens, and the implications for stakeholders' rights and interests.

When ethical dilemmas pose significant challenges, convening ethics committees or advisory panels can provide valuable perspectives and guidance. These bodies, composed of individuals with diverse expertise and backgrounds, offer a forum for in-depth analysis and deliberation, ensuring that a broad range informs decisions of insights and considerations. Furthermore, the documentation of these deliberations and their outcomes serves as a record of decision-making processes and a resource for future reference, contributing to the organization's collective ethical intelligence.

Promoting Transparency and Accountability

Transparency and accountability stand as pillars of ethical AI, ensuring that AI initiatives are conducted in a manner that is open to scrutiny and aligned with societal values. Promoting transparency involves clear communication about the objectives, methodologies, and outcomes of AI projects and the ethical considerations that inform them. This openness extends to sharing datasets, algorithms, and decision-making processes, where feasible, facilitating external review and validation.

On the other hand, accountability encompasses mechanisms for monitoring compliance with ethical standards, reporting on ethical performance, and addressing instances of ethical lapses or failures. This accountability is operationalized through establishing clear responsibilities for ethical oversight, implementing reporting and grievance mechanisms, and enforcing corrective measures when necessary. Moreover, the commitment to accountability is reinforced through regular audits and assessments of AI practices, ensuring that ethical standards are proclaimed and practiced.

In navigating the AI revolution, the cultivation of ethical leadership and the establishment of robust ethical frameworks emerge as critical endeavors. These ensure that the march towards technological innovation is guided by a steadfast commitment to societal well-being and moral responsibility. Through the development and implementation of these frameworks, the proactive role of leaders in ethical governance, the rigorous addressing of ethical dilemmas, and the promotion of transparency and accountability, organizations can harness the transformative potential of AI while upholding the highest standards of ethical integrity.

LEADING BY EXAMPLE: AI ADOPTION STARTS AT THE TOP

Personal Engagement with AI

In the crucible of AI-driven transformation, the impetus for change must emanate from the apex of organizational leadership. The active engagement of leaders with AI technologies is not merely a symbolic gesture but a profound demonstration of their commitment to understanding and leveraging these tools. This engagement requires leaders to not only acquaint themselves with the theoretical underpinnings of AI but also immerse themselves in its practical application. By navigating the functionalities of AI systems firsthand, leaders gain invaluable insights into their operational capabilities and the challenges inherent in their integration. This hands-on approach equips them with the knowledge to make informed decisions regarding AI investments and articulate these technologies' value to their teams with authenticity and conviction. Furthermore, it allows them to critically evaluate the potential of AI to drive strategic outcomes and to identify opportunities for its application across various facets of the business.

Demonstrating Commitment

Demonstrating a leader's commitment to AI adoption is a multifaceted endeavor that extends beyond verbal endorsements to encompass strategic actions and investment decisions. This commitment is manifest in allocating financial and human resources to AI initiatives, signaling to the organization and its stakeholders the strategic importance accorded to AI. By championing AI projects and advocating for their prioritization within the organizational agenda, leaders underscore AI's critical role in shaping the business's future trajectory. Moreover, public endorsements of AI through external communications, participation in industry forums, or sharing of success stories reinforce the organization's position as a forward-thinking entity committed to leveraging AI for innovation and competitive advantage. These public affirmations elevate the organization's stature in the marketplace and galvanize internal constituents, fostering an environment ripe for AI-driven transformation.

Leading Change

The orchestration of organizational change initiatives to embrace AI is a nuanced process that demands strategic foresight and empathetic leadership. Recognizing the multifaceted dimensions of change—cultural, operational, and technological aspects—leaders must adopt a holistic approach to change management.

This approach entails articulating a clear vision for AI adoption, delineating the anticipated benefits and the strategic imperatives driving the initiative. Equally important is cultivating an organizational culture receptive to AI, characterized by openness to experimentation, a willingness to learn from failures, and an agility to adapt to evolving AI landscapes. Leaders must navigate the resistance often accompanying transformative changes, addressing concerns and misconceptions through transparent communication and inclusive dialogue. By involving employees in the AI adoption process, soliciting their input, and addressing their apprehensions, leaders can foster a sense of ownership and commitment to the AI journey. Furthermore, establishing support structures, including training programs and mentorship opportunities, ensures that employees have the skills and confidence to engage with AI technologies, thereby mitigating resistance and enhancing the likelihood of successful AI integration.

Case Studies of Leadership in AI

The landscape of AI adoption is replete with exemplars of visionary leaders who have successfully navigated their organizations through the intricacies of AI transformation. One such leader helmed a multinational corporation in the logistics sector, recognizing early on the potential of AI to revolutionize supply chain management. Under their stewardship, the organization embarked on a comprehensive AI strategy encompassing the deployment of predictive analytics for demand forecasting, integrating autonomous vehicles into logistics operations, and utilizing AI-powered optimization algorithms to enhance route planning. This leader championed these initiatives within the organization and actively engaged with AI technologies, working closely with the AI teams to understand their functionalities and potential impacts. Their unwavering commitment to AI adoption was further demonstrated through substantial investments in AI research and development, partnerships with leading AI startups, and establishing an AI innovation lab. The success of these initiatives, marked by significant improvements in operational efficiency, cost savings, and customer satisfaction, stands as a testament to the transformative power of AI and the pivotal role of leadership in driving its adoption.

In another instance, a leader in the healthcare sector spearheaded the adoption of AI technologies to enhance patient care and streamline clinical operations. Recognizing the capacity of AI to analyze vast datasets and derive insights that could inform clinical decision-making, this leader initiated a collaboration with a leading AI research institution. Through this partnership, the organization developed AI-driven diagnostic tools that significantly improved the accuracy and speed of disease detection. The leader's active involvement in the project, from conceptualization to deployment, and their efforts to foster a culture of innovation within the organization catalyzed a paradigm shift in how clinical services were delivered. By demonstrating a profound commitment to leveraging AI for patient benefit, this leader propelled the organization to the forefront of medical innovation and inspired a culture of continuous improvement and technological exploration.

Through these case studies, the critical importance of leadership in AI adoption is unequivocally underscored. Leaders who engage personally with AI technologies, demonstrate unwavering commitment through strategic actions, adeptly lead organizational change initiatives, and inspire their teams through their example are instrumental in harnessing AI's transformative potential. Their journeys illuminate the path for others, showcasing the indelible impact of visionary leadership in steering organizations toward a future augmented by artificial intelligence.

EMPOWERING TEAMS FOR AI INNOVATION AND SUCCESS

In the intricate weave of the modern corporate fabric, the cultivation of teams equipped to navigate the nuances of artificial intelligence (AI) marks a pivotal shift in the paradigms of innovation and collaboration. The essence of this transformation lies not merely in the aggregation of individuals with technical prowess but in the orchestration of collective intellect and creativity geared towards leveraging AI as a catalyst for groundbreaking solutions. This process entails a meticulous strategy that encapsulates the empowerment of teams, the fostering of cross-functional synergy, the nurturing of a collaborative ethos, and the acknowledgment of AI-driven ingenuity.

Creating Empowered AI Teams

The constitution of empowered AI teams transcends traditional constructs, demanding an alchemy that blends diverse skills, perspectives, and expertise. At the core of this endeavor is the strategic selection of team members, a process that values cognitive diversity as much as technical skills, recognizing that the most innovative solutions often emanate from the confluence of varied thought processes. Empowerment further entails the provision of resources and tools that unlock the potential of AI technologies, coupled with the autonomy to explore, experiment, and even fail. This environment, rich in trust and devoid of fear, cultivates a mindset of exploration that is critical for AI innovation. Leaders must act not as overseers but as enablers, offering guidance and support while championing the creative freedom that fuels ingenuity.

Cross-Functional AI Initiatives

Integrating AI into business operations underscores the necessity for cross-functional teams, where integrating insights from different domains fosters a holistic approach to problem-solving. This cross-pollination of ideas ensures that AI initiatives are technically sound and deeply aligned with business objectives, user needs, and market dynamics. A successful cross-functional AI team functions as a microcosm of the organization, mirroring its complexity and aspirations and serving as a crucible for solutions that resonate with the broader strategic vision. The orchestration of such teams requires adept leadership, capable of bridging silos and cultivating a shared sense of purpose that transcends departmental boundaries.

Fostering a Collaborative Environment

The bedrock of innovation, particularly in AI, is a collaborative environment that encourages sharing knowledge, insights, and learning. This collaboration is not confined to formal meetings or designated projects. Still, it permeates the daily interactions within the organization, fostering a culture where every conversation can spark an idea, and every challenge is viewed as a canvas for innovation. Achieving this level of collaboration requires a deliberate effort to dismantle hierarchical barriers and foster open communication channels. It involves the creation of platforms and forums where team members can share their AI experiences and insights from successes and setbacks and collectively brainstorm solutions. Such an environment accelerates the pace of learning and innovation and strengthens the bonds within the team, building a foundation of mutual respect and understanding.

Recognizing and Rewarding AI Innovation

In the journey of AI-driven transformation, the recognition and reward of innovation serve as powerful catalysts, fueling motivation and reinforcing the value placed on creative endeavors. This acknowledgment goes beyond mere accolades, encompassing a tangible appreciation for the contributions of team members to the AI initiatives. It could manifest in various forms, from formal awards and promotions to further learning and development opportunities, each tailored to affirm the individual's role in fostering innovation. More importantly, this recognition is not reserved for successful outcomes alone but extends to the innovation process, celebrating the courage to venture into the unknown, the resilience to navigate setbacks, and the collaborative spirit that drives collective achievements. Such acknowledgment bolsters ongoing engagement and elevates the organizational ethos, highlighting a commitment to innovation and a recognition of the human ingenuity that powers AI success.

In synthesizing these elements, the empowerment of teams for AI innovation and success emerges as a multifaceted strategy grounded in diversity, autonomy, collaboration, and recognition. It acknowledges AI's transformative potential, leveraged through the collective capabilities and creativity of empowered teams. This approach accelerates the pace of AI innovation. It cultivates an organizational culture where exploring AI's possibilities becomes a shared endeavor, imbued with a sense of purpose and possibility.

As we transition from the discussions of empowering teams and fostering a culture of innovation and collaboration, it's evident that the journey of integrating AI into the heart of business operations is both complex and rewarding. The insights gleaned from this exploration underscore the pivotal role of leadership in navigating this transformation, the strategic empowerment of teams, and the cultivation of an environment that values and thrives on innovation. This narrative, woven with the threads of empowerment, collaboration, and recognition, serves as a prologue to the evolving story of AI in business, guiding us toward the next chapter, where we delve deeper into the practicalities and potentials of AI applications.

DEVELOPING AI TALENT WITHIN YOUR ORGANIZATION

A gardener does not merely plant seeds and wait for them to grow; they assess the soil, provide nutrients, prune, and shape the garden to create a harmonious landscape. Similarly, fostering AI talent within an organization requires a strategic assessment of the current landscape, understanding where the fertile grounds lie and where the soil may be barren. It's a meticulous process that involves identifying existing skills, benchmarking against industry standards, and tailoring learning pathways that align with individual aspirations and organizational goals. This nurturing approach ensures that talent grows and thrives, adapting to the evolving demands of AI technologies and methodologies.

CONDUCTING A SKILLS AUDIT

Initiating a skills audit is akin to the gardener assessing the soil; it's about understanding the current state of play. This process involves systematically reviewing the team's existing capabilities and pinpointing where the knowledge reservoirs are deep and where they run dry. A skills audit, therefore, becomes the first step in mapping out a strategy for AI talent development. It involves surveys, one-on-one interviews, and performance data analysis to overview the team's strengths and weaknesses comprehensively. The outcome of this audit is a clear picture, not dissimilar to a heat map, highlighting areas ripe for development and those already flourishing.

Benchmarking Against Industry Standards

In the fast-paced world of AI, keeping up with industry standards is paramount. Benchmarking against these standards is about staying afloat and leading the way. This process involves a thorough analysis of industry reports, active participation in industry forums, and engagement with AI thought leaders to gain insights into the necessary skills and competencies. For instance, understanding how your team measures up against this capability is crucial if predictive analytics is becoming a norm in the financial industry. This benchmarking exercise highlights skill gaps and provides a roadmap for achieving competitive parity or gaining an advantage.

Tailoring Learning Pathways

Once the terrain is understood and the benchmarks set, the next step is to tailor learning pathways for team members. This approach recognizes that one size does not fit all; each individual has unique learning needs, preferences, and career aspirations. Personalized learning pathways may involve a mix of online courses for foundational knowledge, hands-on experience workshops, and real-world application project assignments. For instance, a team member with a solid statistical background but limited machine learning experience might embark on a learning path that includes an advanced machine learning course, followed by a collaborative project that applies these new skills to a business problem.

Leveraging Internal Talent

Every organization harbors a wealth of untapped potential. Recognizing and harnessing this internal talent is a strategic way to bridge AI skill gaps. This process involves identifying transferable skills—such as analytical thinking, problem-solving, and adaptability—that can be channeled into AI roles. For example, an analyst with expertise in data visualization possesses a foundational skill set that, with additional training in machine learning, could be transitioned into a valuable AI role. This approach addresses skill gaps and provides career development opportunities for employees, enhancing job satisfaction and retention, making it a win-win strategy for your organization.

Interactive Element: AI Skills Development Planner

For a structured and strategic approach to developing AI talent within your organization, consider implementing the 'AI Skills Development Planner.' This tool allows team members to input their current skills, identify areas for development, and choose from personalized learning pathways that align with their career aspirations and the organization's AI objectives. The planner, which can integrate with industry benchmarks and learning resources, offers a dynamic, user-friendly interface for navigating the complexities of AI skill development. A tracking feature enables individuals and leaders to monitor progress, celebrate achievements, and adjust pathways as goals evolve, making it a valuable resource in your talent development strategy.

In navigating the development of AI talent, the strategic, thoughtful approach outlined ensures that teams are not only prepared for the challenges of today but are also primed to lead in the AI-driven landscapes of tomorrow. Through a meticulous process of auditing, benchmarking, personalizing learning, and harnessing internal talent, organizations can cultivate a garden of AI capabilities that is both diverse and robust, ready to thrive in the ever-changing ecosystem of technological innovation.

TRAINING AND UPSKILLING: CREATING AN AI-SAVVY WORKFORCE

In the dynamic realm of artificial intelligence, the metamorphosis of a workforce into a collective that not only comprehends but excels in AI applications demands a meticulous orchestration of resources and initiatives. The curation of AI learning resources thus becomes a pivotal endeavor. It involves a keen assessment of the diverse learning styles that permeate any organization, from the visual learner, enticed by diagrams and flowcharts, to the kinetic learner, who finds clarity in hands-on experimentation. The confluence of online courses that offer the flexibility to learn at one's pace, workshops that provide the immediacy of practical application, and seminars that foster a milieu of discussion and exchange cater to this diversity. This curated collection is not static but evolves, mirroring AI technologies and methodologies advancements. It's akin to an alchemist's Lab, where the right combination of elements can transform base metals into gold, transmuting basic knowledge into profound expertise.

Embedding a culture of continuous learning within an organization transcends the mere provision of resources. It is about creating an ecosystem where curiosity thrives, where the pursuit of knowledge is not mandated but woven into one's daily routines. This culture is cultivated not through edicts but through exemplars; leaders who exhibit an unquenchable thirst for knowledge inspire their teams to do the same. It's about celebrating the quest for understanding, incentivizing achievement, and the journey towards it. Regular 'AI Days, where team members can share insights, explore new AI trends, and present personal projects, act as milestones in this culture, reinforcing the value placed on continuous improvement and lifelong learning.

Measuring the progress of training programs and their impact on AI initiatives introduces a tangible dimension to this endeavor. It shifts the narrative from participation to transformation, where the effectiveness of learning interventions is gauged not just by course completion rates but by their influence on work performance and project outcomes. Advanced analytics tools provide:

- A granular view of learning paths.
- Highlighting patterns of engagement.
- Areas of proficiency.
- Zones needing further exploration.

These insights enable a dynamic adjustment of learning programs, ensuring they remain aligned with individual growth and organizational objectives. The metrics thus gleaned serve as a compass, guiding the strategic direction of training efforts towards areas of maximum impact.

The chronicles of companies that have successfully upskilled their workforce for AI reveal a tapestry of strategies and outcomes. A notable narrative involves a financial institution that embarked on an ambitious plan to imbue its workforce with AI and data analytics skills. Recognizing the diverse learning needs of its employees, the company deployed a multi-pronged approach, integrating online learning platforms with in-house workshops and innovation challenges. The initiative was not a solitary endeavor but coupled with a mentorship program that paired novices with AI experts within the organization. This symbiotic relationship between learning and application bore fruit, culminating in a series of AI-driven projects that ranged from fraud detection algorithms to customer service chatbots. The success of these projects underscored the upskilling initiative's efficacy and heralded a cultural shift towards innovation and continuous learning.

In another instance, a technology firm grappling with the fast-paced evolution of AI instituted a 'Learning Lab' - a dedicated space for experimentation, learning, and cross-disciplinary collaboration. The Lab became the crucible for innovation, where team members, irrespective of their departmental affiliations, congregated to explore AI applications, share knowledge, and develop prototypes. The firm complemented this physical space with a digital platform that offered curated AI learning resources personalized to match its employees' skill levels and interests. The impact was profound; within a year, the firm witnessed a significant uptick in the number of AI projects initiated, a marked improvement in problem-solving capabilities, and a noticeable enhancement in team collaboration. These outcomes were not mere byproducts but the direct result of a strategic emphasis on upskilling continuous learning and a culture that prized innovation and knowledge sharing.

In crafting an AI-savvy workforce, the strategic curation of learning resources, fostering a culture imbued with curiosity and continuous improvement, the meticulous measurement of progress and impact, and the inspiration drawn from success stories merge to form a robust framework. This framework is not static but dynamic, responsive to the evolving landscapes of AI and the workforce's diverse needs. It is a testament to the belief that in the journey towards AI proficiency, the organization that learns together grows together and, in doing so, shapes its destiny in the age of artificial intelligence.

ATTRACTING TOP AI TALENT: RECRUITMENT STRATEGIES

In the kinetic field of artificial intelligence, the magnetism of an organization in the eyes of potential talent can often be the pivot on which the race for innovation turns. The allure of an entity, especially in the AI domain, is predicated not just on the vibrancy of its projects but significantly on the narratives it crafts around the roles it seeks to fill, the vibrancy of its presence in digital and social realms, the strength of its brand as a beacon of AI innovation, and the depth of its connections within the academic cradle of emerging talent.

Crafting Compelling AI Role Descriptions

Clarity and inspiration must intertwine in the meticulous crafting of role descriptions for AI positions, painting a picture of the immediate responsibilities and sketching the broader strokes of impact and growth opportunities. This narrative must articulate how the role fits within the grand tapestry of the organization's mission, how it contributes to cutting-edge AI development, and how it provides a path for professional evolution and mastery. The role description becomes a story where potential candidates see not a job but a calling, a chance to contribute to projects that redefine boundaries and grow in ways that traditional roles do not permit. Including testimonials from current team members, detailing their growth and accomplishments within the organization, adds a layer of authenticity and aspiration, transforming the role description from a mere listing of requirements to an invitation to a professional odyssey.

Leveraging Social Media and Networking

The digital age has transformed social media platforms and professional networking events into fertile grounds for talent acquisition, particularly in AI. An organization's presence on these platforms, characterized by engaging content that highlights innovative projects, team achievements, and insights into the AI technologies being explored, serves as a beacon for top talent. This content strategy should aim not only to inform but to engage, initiating conversations around AI topics, inviting commentary, and fostering a community of AI enthusiasts. Networking events, both virtual and physical, present opportunities to connect with this community in real time to share insights, challenges, and visions for the future of AI. These interactions, enriched with genuine enthusiasm and curiosity, lay the groundwork for relationships that can evolve into recruitment opportunities, drawing talent toward the organization through a shared passion for AI innovation.

Building an Employer Brand in AI

Cultivating an employer brand recognized for its pioneering work in AI is a strategic endeavor that extends beyond marketing into the core of an organization's identity. This brand must embody a commitment to pushing AI's frontiers, ethical practices in AI development, and fostering an environment where innovation thrives. Through a consistent narrative across all channels—be it the company website, social media platforms, industry publications, or speaking engagements at technology conferences—this brand narrative must resonate. It must tell a story of challenges embraced, boundaries pushed, and a future being shaped at the intersection of AI and human ingenuity. This narrative instills a sense of purpose for potential candidates, aligning their personal aspirations for impact and growth with the organization's mission, thereby transforming the employer brand into a magnet for top AI talent.

Partnering with Educational Institutions

The symbiotic relationship between organizations and the academic crucibles of AI talent—universities and coding boot camps—offers a strategic conduit for talent acquisition. These partnerships, nurtured through collaborative research projects, guest lectures by company experts, and internships, serve as bridges that connect the theoretical underpinnings of AI learned in academia with the practical challenges of its application in the industry. For students and recent graduates, these interactions demystify the professional world of AI, presenting a glimpse into the projects and problems that their skills can help solve. For organizations, these partnerships provide early access to emerging talent, individuals who bring fresh perspectives and the latest academic insights into AI. This relationship, cultivated with mutual respect and a shared commitment to advancing the field of AI, becomes a pipeline for future talent, ensuring that the organization remains at the forefront of innovation with a team representing the best and brightest in the field.

In the domain of AI, where the pace of innovation is relentless and the competition for talent fierce, the strategies outlined above serve as the foundation for attracting top professionals. From the articulate crafting of role descriptions that inspire, through the strategic use of social media and networking to engage to the cultivation of a brand that resonates with a commitment to AI innovation and the nurturing of partnerships with educational institutions—the approach to recruitment becomes a reflection of the organization's vision for the future of AI. It's a vision that seeks to lead in the development of AI technologies and build a community of professionals who are not just employees but pioneers at the forefront of artificial intelligence.

CULTIVATING A COLLABORATIVE ENVIRONMENT FOR AI INNOVATION

The soil from which the spirit of collaboration richly fertilizes the seeds of AI innovation sprout. This spirit, transcending the traditional confines of departments and specialties, weaves a tapestry of collective intelligence, a prerequisite for groundbreaking advancements in artificial intelligence. The cultivation of such an ecosystem, where ideas flow freely, and synergies are encouraged and actively pursued, becomes the bedrock upon which AI initiatives flourish.

Promoting Cross-Departmental Projects

The inception of cross-departmental projects embodies the essence of collaborative innovation. By dismantling the invisible walls that often segregate departments, organizations enable a confluence of diverse perspectives, each adding depth and dimension to AI initiatives. Picture a scenario where the marketing team's insights on consumer behavior merge with the tech team's prowess in machine learning algorithms, coalescing into an AI-driven tool that predicts consumer trends and crafts highly personalized marketing campaigns. Such projects necessitate a shift in mindset, from viewing departments as standalone entities to considering them integral pieces of a larger puzzle, each contributing a unique piece to the AI mosaic. The role of leadership in facilitating this shift cannot be understated; it requires a commitment to fostering a culture where collaboration is not just an option but a norm.

Creating AI Innovation Labs

Establishing AI innovation labs is a tangible manifestation of an organization's dedication to nurturing collaborative AI exploration. These labs, equipped with the latest technologies and staffed by multidisciplinary teams, become arenas of experimentation where boundaries are pushed and the status quo is challenged. Imagine these labs as incubators, where ideas, no matter how nascent, are given the space to evolve, guided by the team's collective expertise. The benefits of such dedicated spaces extend beyond the immediate outcomes of the projects they house; they serve as beacons, attracting talent within the organization, drawn by the opportunity to be part of something truly transformative. Furthermore, these labs become focal points for organizational learning as the insights and knowledge generated within their confines percolate throughout the organization, elevating the collective AI acumen.

Fostering Open Communication

The cornerstone of effective collaboration, particularly in the realm of AI innovation, is the establishment of open communication channels. These channels, free from hierarchical constraints and bureaucratic red tape, encourage the uninhibited exchange of ideas, feedback, and constructive criticism. It's about creating an environment where the intern feels as empowered as the department head to voice an idea, where feedback is solicited and valued, and where every project is viewed as a learning opportunity. This openness transforms the process of AI development from a series of tasks to be completed into a collaborative journey, where each milestone, whether a breakthrough or a setback, is shared and learned from. Implementing regular AI forums, where teams can present projects, share challenges, and seek input, exemplifies this philosophy, turning communication into a tool for innovation.

Recognizing and Rewarding Collaboration

The recognition and reward of collaborative efforts in AI projects underscore their value to the organization. It's an acknowledgment that the whole is greater than the sum of its parts and that when teams come together, their combined efforts yield outcomes that individual endeavors could not. This recognition can take many forms, from awards celebrating collaborative achievements to incentives designed specifically for teams that exemplify cross-functional synergy. More than just tokens of appreciation, these rewards serve a dual purpose. They not only celebrate the achievements of the present but also set a precedent for the future, signaling to the organization that collaboration is not just encouraged; it's celebrated. A case in point involves a multinational corporation that instituted an 'AI Innovation Award,' presented annually to teams demonstrating exceptional collaborative spirit and innovation in AI projects. The award, accompanied by significant professional development opportunities for team members, became a coveted accolade, driving teams across the organization to seek out and embrace collaborative projects.

In the realm of artificial intelligence, where the complexities and challenges are as vast as the potential rewards, the role of a collaborative environment cannot be overstated. The true power of AI is unlocked in the melding of minds, the fusion of diverse perspectives, and the collective pursuit of innovation. Through the promotion of cross-departmental projects, the creation of spaces dedicated to AI exploration, the fostering of open communication, and the recognition of collaborative efforts, organizations can cultivate an ecosystem where AI innovation not only takes root but thrives, propelled by the shared vision and collective effort of its people.

SUCCESS STORIES: BUILDING WORLD-CLASS AI TEAMS

The landscape of artificial intelligence is dotted with entities that have carved niches of excellence, setting benchmarks that resonate across sectors. Through a blend of strategic foresight, leadership understanding, and a relentless pursuit of innovation, these organizations have sculpted AI teams that are not merely functional but exemplary. The narratives of their ascension offer a rich repository of insights, strategies, and lessons that serve as waypoints for others aspiring to cultivate similar echelons of AI prowess.

In one notable example, a tech conglomerate renowned for its AI-driven solutions underwent a transformative journey to assemble an AI team that today stands as a paragon of innovation. The initial phase was marked by an audacious recruitment strategy, targeting not just seasoned AI professionals but also prodigious talents from academia and parallel industries. This approach was predicated on the belief that a fusion of diverse experiences and expertise would catalyze a culture of innovation where unconventional ideas are not outliers but the norm. The conglomerate complemented this strategy with an immersive onboarding experience designed to acclimatize new recruits to the company's ethos, projects, and expectations, thereby ensuring a seamless melding of talents into the organizational fabric.

Parallel to recruitment, the leadership instituted a dynamic mentorship program, pairing novices with seasoned AI veterans. This initiative was not a mere transfer of knowledge but a bidirectional exchange, where fresh perspectives challenged established norms, and tacit knowledge was distilled into actionable insights. The mentorship program, thus, became a crucible for nurturing AI talent, fostering a milieu where learning was continuous and collaborative.

Another exemplar of AI team excellence emerged from a healthcare startup that leveraged AI to revolutionize diagnostic methodologies. The startup's success was anchored in its ability to create a collaborative environment transcending traditional departmental barriers. Cross-functional teams comprising AI experts, clinicians, and data scientists coalesced around shared objectives, driving innovations seamlessly blending clinical acumen with AI precision. This collaborative spirit was further fueled by regular ideation sessions and open forums where team members, irrespective of rank or tenure, could table ideas, challenge assumptions, and co-create solutions. The result was a series of breakthrough AI models that significantly enhanced diagnostic accuracy, underscoring the potency of collaboration in driving AI innovation.

From these narratives, a constellation of lessons emerges, chief among them being the pivotal role of leadership in cultivating AI talent. Leaders in these organizations acted as architects of culture, laying the foundations upon which AI excellence was built. They recognized that creating world-class AI teams was not a serendipitous event but a deliberate act marked by strategic recruitment, intentional mentorship, and fostering an inclusive, collaborative culture. These leaders also understood that sustaining AI team excellence required not just the maintenance of the status quo but an ongoing investment in learning and development, ensuring that the team's skills and knowledge evolved in tandem with advancements in AI.

Strategies for sustained success in these organizations were multifaceted, intertwining the development of individual competencies with the cultivation of a team ethos that celebrated innovation, diversity, and inclusivity. Investment in state-of-the-art AI labs and research initiatives ensured that teams had access to the tools and resources necessary to push the boundaries of what is possible. Moreover, a transparent communication ethos ensured that AI successes and failures were shared learning experiences, reinforcing a culture where risk-taking was not feared but encouraged.

In synthesizing these insights, the message is unmistakable: constructing world-class AI teams is an exercise in strategic foresight, leadership, and a steadfast commitment to fostering an environment where talent thrives. It's a narrative that transcends the mere acquisition of skills, delving into creating ecosystems where innovation is not just possible but inevitable. As we transition from these stories of triumph and the lessons they impart, the path forward beckons with the promise of new challenges and the perpetual quest for innovation in AI. It's a journey that demands not just the mastery of technology but the cultivation of teams poised to redefine the frontiers of what AI can achieve.

LEVERAGING AI FOR TEAM DYNAMICS AND COLLABORATION

In the heart of a bustling city, a bridge spans a once-uncrossable river, linking neighborhoods and facilitating a flow of ideas, commerce, and community. This bridge does more than connect two points; it transforms the landscape, fostering opportunities for collaboration that were previously inconceivable. In much the same way, artificial intelligence has emerged as a pivotal bridge in the modern business environment, linking disparate elements of the workforce, enhancing communication, and seeding unprecedented levels of collaboration. This chapter focuses on AI's instrumental role in redefining team dynamics, mainly through tools that streamline collaboration, making what was once a tangled web of processes a seamless, integrated flow of productivity and innovation.

AI TOOLS THAT FACILITATE TEAM COLLABORATION

Collaboration Platforms with AI Features

In today's digital-first world, collaboration platforms have become the backbone of team interactions, transcending geographical limitations and fostering a cohesive work environment. AI has injected these platforms with a new level of intelligence and efficiency. For instance, platforms now boast AI-driven features like smart notifications, prioritizing messages based on urgency and relevance, and ensuring team members stay focused on what truly matters. Imagine a scenario where a project manager receives an alert for a critical update on a high-priority project while non-urgent notifications are subtly deprioritized. This nuanced approach to communication underscores the transformative impact of AI on team collaboration, ensuring that the correct information reaches the right person at the right time, thus optimizing workflow and productivity.

AI for Meeting Efficiency

Meetings, the linchpin of collaboration, often need to improve efficiency, ranging from off-topic discussions to unclear conclusions. AI tools are revolutionizing this aspect of teamwork by offering real-time meeting summaries, action items, and follow-up tasks, all generated with a precision that human note-takers might struggle to match. This AI capability ensures that meetings are not just sessions of discussion but pivotal moments of action and clarity. For businesses, this means ending the all-too-common post-meeting scramble, where participants try to recall discussion points and next steps. Instead, AI provides a clear roadmap of tasks and responsibilities directly in the meeting platform and is accessible to all participants.

Enhancing Remote Work

The shift to remote work, accelerated by global circumstances, brought to light the challenges of connectivity and engagement outside the traditional office. AI tools are pivotal in bridging these gaps, offering solutions replicating and enhancing the in-office experience. Through AI-driven analysis of work patterns, these tools can suggest optimal times for team check-ins, predict potential project bottlenecks, and even recommend breaks when productivity wanes. This insight into the rhythm of remote work helps teams balance productivity and well-being, ensuring that the digital workspace is efficient and humane.

Integrating AI into Existing Tools

The power of AI in collaboration often shines brightest not in standalone applications but in its integration into existing tools and systems. The key is seamless integration, from email clients that use AI to sort and prioritize messages to project management tools that predict project timelines and identify risks. This approach minimizes the learning curve and disruption associated with adopting new technologies, allowing teams to benefit from AI enhancements within familiar environments. For businesses considering this integration, the focus should be on identifying areas where AI can have the most immediate and impactful effect on productivity and then working with AI solution providers to tailor these integrations to their specific workflows and needs.

Visual Element: The AI Collaboration Ecosystem Infographic

To encapsulate the diverse array of AI tools and their applications in enhancing team collaboration, an infographic titled "The AI

Collaboration Ecosystem" provides a visual overview. This infographic categorizes AI tools according to their primary function—communication optimization, meeting efficiency, remote work enhancement, and system integration—offering examples of each and illustrating how they interconnect to create a comprehensive ecosystem. For teams and leaders, this visual guide serves as an introduction to the potential of AI in collaboration and a roadmap for integrating these tools into their daily operations.

In the landscape of modern business, where agility and innovation are paramount, AI is a transformative force, reshaping how teams communicate, collaborate, and achieve collective success. Through intelligent collaboration platforms, meeting efficiency tools, enhancements for remote work, and strategic integration into existing systems, AI bridges gaps, aligns efforts, and illuminates paths forward. For leaders aiming to harness the full potential of their teams, integrating AI into collaboration strategies offers a bridge to a future where productivity, innovation, and team dynamics are optimized and reimagined.

ENHANCING CREATIVITY: AI'S ROLE IN THE CREATIVE PROCESS

In the realm of invention and design, artificial intelligence emerges not merely as a tool but as a profound collaborator, offering avenues for creative exploration that push the boundaries of conventional thought. The partnership between human ingenuity and AI's computational prowess propels the creative process into uncharted territories, where the synthesis of ideas and the speed of experimentation unfold at a pace once deemed unattainable. This symbiosis, marked by the fusion of intuitive human creativity and AI's analytical capabilities, paves the way for a renaissance in innovation, design, and content creation.

The role of AI as a creative partner is both sublime and transformative, serving as a catalyst that ignites the spark of creativity in realms where stagnation looms. In instances where the creative well runs dry, AI tools emerge as a beacon of inspiration, offering fresh perspectives derived from data patterns invisible to the human eye. These tools, through algorithms that sift through vast repositories of artistic and design precedents, can suggest novel combinations of colors, forms, and themes, thus providing a springboard for creative leaps. For example, designers grappling with the challenge of creating a visual identity for a brand might leverage AI to generate a palette of colors and motifs that resonate with the brand's ethos, distilled from an analysis of cultural trends and consumer preferences.

Moreover, AI's capacity to expedite the experimentation phase of the creative process is unparalleled. Prototyping, a critical yet often time-consuming stage in design and content development, benefits significantly from AI's ability to rapidly model and test variations, thereby compressing the timeline from concept to final product. This acceleration is not trivial; it represents a seismic shift in how creative professionals iterate and refine their work, enabling a fluidity and adaptability that were once constrained by logistical limitations. Consider digital marketing, where content creators might employ AI to swiftly generate and test many ad copy variations, analyzing performance in real-time to refine messaging that resonates with target audiences.

In design and content creation, AI stands as both muse and artisan, facilitating the genesis of initial concepts and the meticulous refinement of final products. The application of generative AI models in graphic design, for instance, allows for creating innovative visuals that are deeply aligned with specific aesthetic criteria, transcending traditional design paradigms. Similarly, in content creation, AI tools adept at understanding natural language can produce draft articles, scripts, and marketing copy, which, while requiring human oversight and final touches, significantly streamline the content development process.

Yet, embracing AI in the creative process necessitates a conscientious examination of ethical considerations, notably copyright and originality. The intersection of AI-generated content and intellectual property rights introduces a complex web of ethical dilemmas as the distinction between creator and tool becomes blurred. Navigating this landscape requires a nuanced understanding of copyright laws and a commitment to ensuring that AI, as a facilitator of creativity, does not inadvertently become a source of infringement. This delicate balance between leveraging AI for creative enhancement and safeguarding the sanctity of original work underscores the need for clear guidelines and ethical frameworks within which AI's role in the creative process is delineated.

Furthermore, the question of originality in the context of AI-assisted creation invites a reevaluation of the concept. As AI algorithms draw upon existing works to generate new content, the creative community is prompted to reflect on what constitutes genuine innovation. This reflection is not a rebuke of AI's potential to inspire and expedite creativity but rather an acknowledgment of the collaborative nature of creativity in the digital age. It posits AI as a mirror, reflecting the vast expanse of human creative expression, and as a lens, focusing the infinite possibilities of innovation into tangible forms.

In this era of rapid technological advancement, the fusion of human creativity and artificial intelligence heralds a new chapter in the annals of design, content creation, and artistic expression. As creative professionals and organizations navigate this evolving landscape, the partnership with AI emerges as a profound alliance that augments the creative capacity and challenges and extends the definitions of creativity and innovation. In the dance of ideas and algorithms, a new paradigm of creativity emerges, marked by boundless possibilities, ethical contemplation, and the relentless pursuit of originality and expression.

BREAKING DOWN SILOS: AI AS A BRIDGE BETWEEN DEPARTMENTS

In the intricate web of modern organizational structures, departments often evolve into silos, isolated entities that, while striving toward their specific goals, inadvertently impede the flow of information and innovation across the organization. The advent of artificial intelligence offers a paradigm shift; a means not merely to bridge these divides but to forge a unified entity that thrives on shared knowledge and collaborative effort. In this context, AI emerges as a pivotal force in dismantling these barriers, fostering an environment where cross-functional data sharing becomes the norm, interdepartmental projects the standard, and overcoming traditional barriers a shared objective.

Facilitating Cross-Functional Data Sharing

The lifeblood of any organization in the digital age is data. Yet, the value of this data is often trapped within departmental confines, its potential to inform and transform stifled by the silos that contain it. AI introduces a dynamic shift in this narrative, providing tools and systems that can aggregate, analyze, and disseminate data across the breadth of an organization. This capability ensures that insights gleaned in one corner of the organization can illuminate decisions in another, fostering a culture of informed decision-making and strategic alignment. For instance, marketing insights into customer behavior can inform product development, while finance's budget forecasts can guide marketing strategies, creating a cohesive, data-informed approach to organizational growth.

Encouraging Interdepartmental Projects

The genesis of innovation often lies in the confluence of diverse perspectives. AI catalyzes such innovation, offering platforms and processes that encourage and facilitate interdepartmental collaboration. By leveraging AI-driven project management tools, organizational leaders can initiate and manage projects that draw upon the strengths and insights of multiple departments. This approach enhances the innovation potential of these projects and fosters a sense of unity and shared purpose within the organization. Teams that once operated in isolation begin to see their efforts as part of a larger mosaic, contributing to a holistic vision that transcends departmental boundaries.

Overcoming Departmental Barriers

The barriers between departments, often rooted in historical precedents and entrenched processes, present a formidable challenge to organizational cohesion. With its capacity to streamline processes and enhance communication, AI provides a set of keys to unlock these barriers. Through AI-driven analytics and communication platforms, departments gain insights into each other's workflows, challenges, and objectives, paving the way for a more integrated approach to projects and problem-solving. This transparency does not merely illuminate the workings of disparate teams; it fosters empathy and understanding, laying the groundwork for a collaborative culture that views departmental barriers not as fixtures but as relics of a bygone era.

A narrative that underscores the transformative impact of AI in breaking down silos comes from a global corporation that, faced with the challenge of siloed operations, turned to AI for a solution. The corporation implemented an AI-driven internal platform that mapped each department's skills, projects, and needs, creating a virtual space where employees could seek and offer assistance across traditional boundaries. This platform led to the emergence of cross-functional teams that tackled projects ranging from sustainability initiatives to customer experience enhancements, each drawing on the diverse expertise of the organization. The success of these projects, marked by innovative solutions and enhanced operational efficiency, served as a testament to the power of AI in fostering a culture of collaboration and breaking down the walls that once compartmentalized the organization.

In the realm of modern business, where agility and innovation are the twin pillars of success, the ability to transcend traditional silos and foster a culture of collaboration is not merely an advantage; it is a necessity. Artificial intelligence stands at the forefront of this shift, offering tools, systems, and insights that bridge divides, enhance communication, and promote a unified approach to organizational goals. Through the strategic application of AI, organizations can transform from a collection of isolated entities into a cohesive, dynamic whole, where shared knowledge and collaborative effort drive innovation and growth.

In this new paradigm, AI serves as a bridge between departments and a foundation for a more integrated, innovative, and efficient organization.

FOSTERING AN INCLUSIVE CULTURE THROUGH AI INITIATIVES

In the nuanced tapestry of modern workplaces, the threads of diversity and inclusion weave a pattern rich with the potential for innovation, resilience, and growth. Against this backdrop, artificial intelligence emerges not merely as a technological tool but as a catalyst for cultivating an environment where every individual, regardless of background or ability, finds empowerment and equity. When aligned with principles of diversity and inclusion, the deployment of AI initiatives transcends traditional boundaries, offering a lens through which decision-making processes are refined, development teams are diversified, accessibility is enhanced, and a culture of inclusivity is nurtured.

At the core of leveraging AI to promote diversity and inclusion lies the pivotal challenge of eliminating biases that often permeate decision-making processes. Embedded within algorithms, intentional or unintentional biases can reinforce stereotypes and perpetuate inequalities. The strategic application of AI, however, holds the promise of dismantling these biases, offering a pathway to decisions that are not only data-driven but also equitable. Through sophisticated machine learning models trained on diverse datasets, AI can identify and mitigate biases, ensuring that recruitment, promotion, and project assignment decisions reflect meritocracy and diversity. This transformative approach to decision-making fosters an environment where talent thrives, uninhibited by the constraints of bias, and where diversity is acknowledged and embraced as a source of strength and innovation.

The diversity of AI development teams is a cornerstone in creating inclusive AI tools. A homogenous team, bound by a singular perspective, inadvertently designs solutions that mirror its image, overlooking the rich mosaic of human experience. Conversely, a team that reflects a broad spectrum of backgrounds, experiences, and viewpoints harnesses the power of this diversity to create AI solutions that cater to a wide array of needs and preferences. Such solutions reach a broader audience and resonate on a deeper level, addressing nuances that might otherwise be overlooked. The commitment to diversifying AI teams thus becomes a commitment to inclusivity, ensuring that the tools developed serve and empower the full breadth of human diversity.

AI tools engineered to enhance workplace accessibility underscore the profound impact of technology on creating an environment where individuals with disabilities are not just accommodated but empowered. From voice-activated interfaces that facilitate hands-free interaction to AI-driven applications that translate visual content into audible narratives, these tools dismantle barriers, offering individuals the autonomy to engage with their work on equal footing. Integrating such AI tools into workplace environments signals an organizational commitment to accessibility, affirming the principle that every employee, regardless of physical ability, has the right to participate fully and effectively in the workplace. This commitment extends beyond compliance with legal mandates, embodying a deeper ethos of inclusivity and respect for diversity.

The journey toward building a culture that values inclusivity and leverages AI to support this goal requires more than implementing tools and policies; it demands a shift in mindset. It calls for an environment where ongoing dialogue around diversity, inclusion, and accessibility is encouraged, where feedback loops are established to refine AI initiatives in light of diverse perspectives continually, and where leadership champions the cause of inclusivity, setting a precedent for the organization. In this culture, AI becomes more than a technological asset; it transforms into a partner fostering an environment of understanding, respect, and empowerment.

The commitment to fostering an inclusive culture through AI initiatives is not a solitary endeavor but a collective journey that involves every stakeholder within the organization. From developers who design AI with an eye toward inclusivity to leaders who advocate for diversity and inclusion and employees who embrace and champion the cause, each plays a pivotal role in weaving the fabric of an inclusive workplace. The strategic deployment of AI in this context is both a reflection of and a catalyst for this culture, offering insights that challenge biases, tools that enhance accessibility, and practices that promote diversity.

In this landscape, AI initiatives mirror the organization's commitment to diversity and inclusion. They are a beacon guiding the way toward a future where every individual, irrespective of their background, abilities, or perspectives, finds a place of belonging and an opportunity to thrive. The transformation of workplaces into environments that not only accommodate but celebrate diversity, ensure equity and foster inclusion stands as a testament to the potential of AI to change not just the way we work but also the fabric of our organizational cultures.

CASE STUDY: AI-DRIVEN COLLABORATION IN MULTINATIONAL COMPANIES

Navigating the intricate landscape of multinational corporations reveals a complex matrix of collaboration challenges, magnified by the vast geographical divides and the rich tapestry of cultural variances. These entities grapple with ensuring seamless communication and collaboration among teams scattered across time zones, each embedded in distinct cultural contexts. While a source of strength, the inherent diversity poses unique hurdles in achieving a unified workflow and maintaining the coherence of corporate culture across global offices.

In response to these challenges, a cadre of forward-thinking multinational companies has turned to artificial intelligence as a linchpin for fostering collaboration across their dispersed teams. The initiation of AI solutions within these organizations was not a leap in the dark but a strategic maneuver, underscored by a meticulous assessment of collaboration impediments and the potential of AI to bridge these gaps. One such solution involved the deployment of AI-driven platforms designed to optimize project management and facilitate real-time communication, transcending the barriers imposed by varying time zones.

These platforms employed sophisticated algorithms to analyze the communication patterns and project statuses across global teams, offering predictive insights that preempted bottlenecks and streamlined workflows. Furthermore, natural language processing capabilities enabled real-time translation features, mitigating language barriers and fostering an inclusive environment where ideas flowed freely, unencumbered by linguistic constraints. This innovative approach to utilizing AI to enhance global collaboration marked a significant departure from conventional methods, leveraging technology to knit disparate teams into a cohesive unit.

The outcomes and benefits of implementing these AI solutions were manifold and profound. Companies observed a marked improvement in communication efficiency, with teams able to share ideas and feedback more fluidly, leading to faster decision-making processes. The predictive insights generated by AI-driven platforms enabled project managers to allocate resources more effectively, enhancing productivity and reducing project turnaround time. Moreover, fostering an inclusive environment through real-time translation and culturally sensitive AI algorithms increased employee engagement and satisfaction, as team members felt valued and understood, regardless of their geographical or cultural background.

Innovation, a critical byproduct of these AI-enhanced collaboration efforts, flourished as teams were empowered to share diverse perspectives and co-create solutions without distance or language. The synergy achieved through AI-facilitated collaboration sparked creativity and led to the development of groundbreaking products and services, reinforcing the companies' positions as leaders in their respective industries. This innovation surge underscored AI's transformative potential in redefining collaboration within multinational corporations, turning geographical dispersion and cultural diversity from challenges into assets.

Key takeaways for other organizations looking to harness AI to enhance collaboration across geographically dispersed teams include:

- The importance of a strategic approach to AI integration.
- Focusing on specific collaboration challenges.
- Leveraging AI to address these issues directly.

The necessity of investing in AI solutions that prioritize inclusivity and cultural sensitivity cannot be overstated, as these factors are crucial in fostering a collaborative environment that values and leverages diversity. Additionally, the commitment to continuous innovation in AI applications ensures that collaboration tools evolve with the changing dynamics of global teams, maintaining their relevance and efficacy.

In sum, exploring AI-driven collaboration in multinational companies offers a compelling narrative of how technology can transcend physical and cultural boundaries, transforming challenges into opportunities for enhanced communication, efficiency, and innovation. The strategic deployment of AI facilitates seamless collaboration across disparate teams and cultivates an environment where diversity is celebrated and innovation thrives. As we move forward, the lessons gleaned from these pioneering efforts in leveraging AI for global collaboration provide a blueprint for other organizations seeking to navigate the complexities of the modern business world, where the ability to collaborate effectively across borders and cultures is not just an advantage but a necessity.

As this exploration of AI-driven collaboration in multinational companies draws to a close, it's evident that the journey towards leveraging technology for enhancing teamwork and creativity is both ongoing and dynamic. The insights from these case studies illuminate the path for other organizations, offering a vision of a future where AI bridges geographical and cultural divides and catalyzes innovation and inclusivity. This narrative, rich with the potential of AI to transform the very fabric of collaboration, sets the stage for the next chapter in our exploration of artificial intelligence in the business world, where we delve deeper into the strategic integration of AI across various facets of organizational operations, aiming to unlock new horizons of efficiency, innovation, and growth.

CONCLUSION

As we reach the culmination of our journey together through the pages of this book, it's time to reflect on the transformative path we've embarked upon. From the initial steps of demystifying artificial intelligence to the strategic integration into our daily business operations, navigating ethical considerations, and ultimately leveraging AI for a competitive edge, this exploration has been nothing short of a revelation. As unfolded in these chapters, the narrative of AI empowerment for business leaders illuminates a less-traveled road ripe with opportunities for those daring enough to take the first step.

Throughout our discourse, we've traversed the landscape of generative AI, dissected the jargon clouding the realm of artificial intelligence, and unveiled AI's practical applications for the modern business leader. The essence of this book, distilled into its most potent form, delivers key insights:

- The imperative of aligning AI with your strategic vision.

- Fostering a culture ready for AI innovation.
- The continuous journey of learning and adaptation that AI demands.

For you, the business leaders at the helm of this new era, the main takeaways crystallize into a beacon guiding your voyage through the AI revolution. Understand that AI is not just a technological tool but a strategic ally poised to redefine the way we conceive business models, customer experiences, and operational efficiencies. Its integration can lead to significant cost savings, improved productivity, and enhanced customer satisfaction.

Embrace AI with the confidence of a pioneer venturing into uncharted territories, armed with the knowledge that the power of AI, when harnessed with insight, creativity, and ethical consideration, can catapult your enterprise into realms of unprecedented innovation and success. Remember, understanding AI and its myriad potentials marks only the dawn of this expedition. The true essence of empowerment lies in taking definitive action, experimenting boldly, and adapting your strategies to the evolving landscape of AI applications and outcomes. This requires a commitment to continuous learning and adaptation, as AI is a rapidly evolving field.

As we part ways on this written journey, I urge you not to view this as an ending but as the beginning of your adventure with AI. Start small, yet dream audaciously about the impact AI can wield within your organization. Begin with a pilot project or a small-scale implementation, and gradually expand as you gain confidence and see the benefits. Let the insights and strategies shared in these pages serve as your compass, guiding your steps from theoretical understanding to practical, impactful implementation.

To aid in your ongoing quest for AI mastery, I encourage you to delve into a curated list of resources. Online courses, vibrant communities, and cutting-edge publications stand ready to augment your knowledge and keep you abreast of the latest advancements in AI. These resources are not just tools, but a support system, ready to guide you and provide you with the confidence you need to navigate the complexities of AI implementation. Embrace these tools as your allies in the continuous pursuit of excellence in the age of AI.

In conclusion, let us look forward with optimism to the future of business leadership. In this future, AI and human ingenuity converge to create a tapestry of innovation, ethical progress, and sustainable growth. The era of AI is not on the horizon—it is here, now, inviting us to redefine what's possible. With AI as our steadfast companion, we stand on the precipice of a new dawn for business leadership, one marked by boundless potential and the promise of a future crafted with wisdom, creativity, and ethical foresight.

The journey of a thousand miles begins with a single step. Let that step be yours, encouraged by the knowledge you now hold and the future you can envision. The age of AI awaits, not as a challenge to be feared but as an opportunity to be seized, promising a legacy of innovation and leadership that will echo through the annals of business history. Let us stride forward together into this brave new world.

REFERENCES

Our Artificial Intelligence Client Success Stories | BCG https://www.bcg.com/capabilities/artificial-intelligence/client-success

Economic potential of generative AI https://www.mckinsey.com/capabilities/mckinsey-digital/our-insights/the-economic-potential-of-generative-ai-the-next-productivity-frontier

AI and ethics: Business leaders know it's important, but ... https://fortune.com/2023/11/08/ai-playbook-jobs/

The state of AI in 2023: Generative AI's breakout year https://www.mckinsey.com/capabilities/quantumblack/our-insights/the-state-of-ai-in-2023-generative-ais-breakout-year

AI For Business - 30 Case Studies That Led To Competitive ... https://digitaltransformationskills.com/ai-for-business/

Building the AI-Powered Organization https://hbr.org/2019/07/building-the-ai-powered-organization

Artificial Intelligence: the next frontier in investment ... https://www.deloitte.com/global/en/Industries/financial-services/perspectives/ai-next-frontier-in-investment-management.html

Best Practices in Developing an Enterprise AI Roadmap https://c3.ai/what-is-enterprise-ai/best-practices-in-developing-an-enterprise-ai-roadmap/

AI Readiness Checklist https://www.launchconsulting.com/insights-briefs/printable-checklist-your-free-roadmap-to-ai-readiness

6 AI Implementation Challenges And How To Overcome ... https://elearningindustry.com/ai-implementation-challenges-and-how-to-overcome-them

How AI Can Help Overcome The Challenges Of Legacy Data Integration https://aretecinc.com/how-ai-can-help-overcome-the-challenges-of-legacy-data-integration/

The 20 Best Examples Of Using Artificial Intelligence For Retail Experiences https://www.forbes.com/sites/blakemorgan/2019/03/04/the-20-best-examples-of-using-artificial-intelligence-for-retail-experiences/

Case Study: Walmart's AI-Enhanced Supply Chain Operations https://aiexpert.network/case-study-walmarts-ai-enhanced-supply-chain-operations/

How AI Can Help Leaders Make Better Decisions Under ... https://hbr.org/2023/10/how-ai-can-help-leaders-make-better-decisions-under-pressure

Harnessing Predictive Analytics in Business | WM MSBA https://online.mason.wm.edu/blog/predictive-analytics-in-business

A Unified Framework of Five Principles for AI in Society https://hdsr.mitpress.mit.edu/pub/l0jsh9d1

Best Approaches to Mitigate Bias in AI Models https://innodata.com/best-approaches-to-mitigate-bias-in-ai-models/

AI & the GDPR: Regulating the minds of machines - Linklaters https://www.linklaters.com/en-us/insights/blogs/digilinks/ai-and-the-gdpr-regulating-the-minds-of-machines

Building Transparency into AI Projects https://hbr.org/2022/06/building-transparency-into-ai-projects

AI and cyber security: what you need to know - NCSC.GOV.UK https://www.ncsc.gov.uk/guidance/ai-and-cyber-security-what-you-need-to-know

A survey of artificial intelligence risk assessment ... https://www.trilateralresearch.com/wp-content/uploads/2022/01/A-survey-of-AI-Risk-Assessment-Methodologies-full-report.pdf

14 Cybersecurity Best Practices When Working with AI https://solutionsreview.com/endpoint-security/14-cybersecurity-best-practices-when-working-with-ai/

Data Integrity And AI: Why You Need Both To Power Trusted Business Decisions https://www.forbes.com/sites/forbestechcouncil/2021/12/29/data-integrity-and-ai-why-you-need-both-to-power-trusted-business-decisions/

15 AI tools for business analytics to gain a competitive edge https://www.pluralsight.com/resources/blog/data/15-business-analytics-ai-tools

48 Artificial Intelligence Examples to Know for 2024 https://builtin.com/artificial-intelligence/examples-ai-in-industry

The Future of AI: How AI Is Changing the World https://builtin.com/artificial-intelligence/artificial-intelligence-future

Artificial Intelligence: Implications for Business Strategy https://executive.mit.edu/course/artificial-intelligence/a056g00000URaa3AAD.html

Building a Future-Ready Workforce: The Essential Role of ... https://www.linkedin.com/pulse/building-future-ready-workforce-essential-role-ai-literacy-jamil-rq8xf

A Practical Guide to Building Ethical AI https://hbr.org/2020/10/a-practical-guide-to-building-ethical-ai

How 4 Companies Transformed with Generative AI Adoption https://www.kommunicate.io/blog/how-4-companies-transformed-with-generative-ai-adoption/

Why we must bridge the skills gap to harness the power of AI https://www.weforum.org/agenda/2024/01/to-truly-harness-ai-we-must-close-the-ai-skills-gap/

AI Upskilling: 5 Best Practices to Consider https://trainingindustry.com/articles/workforce-development/ai-upskilling-5-best-practices-to-consider/

AI Case Studies: Success Stories in Talent Acquisition ... https://medium.com/shark-automations/ai-case-studies-success-stories-in-talent-acquisition-transformation-d37c77f87f06

Seven Steps To Establishing An Innovation Culture For AI ... https://www.forbes.com/sites/forbestechcouncil/2023/05/05/seven-steps-to-establishing-an-innovation-culture-for-ai-and-data-services-companies/

14 Best AI Collaboration Tools for Remote Teams ... https://www.taskade.com/blog/ai-collaboration-tools-for-remote-teams/

How Generative AI Can Augment Human Creativity https://hbr.org/2023/07/how-generative-ai-can-augment-human-creativity

Beyond Automation: The Rise of AI-Driven Creativity and ... https://medium.com/@oluwafemidiakhoa/beyond-automation-the-rise-of-ai-driven-creativity-and-ethical-implications-50fea004aac8

How AI Is Helping Companies Break Silos https://sloanreview.mit.edu/article/how-ai-is-helping-companies-break-silos/

UNDERSTANDING GENERATIVE AI FOR BUSINESS LEADERS

DEMYSTIFYING STRATEGIC ADVANTAGE, ETHICAL DEPLOYMENT, AND PRACTICAL INTERGRATION FOR SUCCESS

"Great leaders don't set out to be leaders. They set out to make a difference. It's never about the role—it's always about the goal."

— LISA HAISHA

People who give without expectation live longer, happier lives and make more money. So if we've got a shot at that during our time together, darn it, I'm gonna try.

To make that happen, I have a question for you...

Would you help someone you've never met, even if you never got credit for it?

Who is this person you ask? They are like you. Or, at least, like you used to be. Less experienced, wanting to make a difference, and needing help, but not sure where to look.

Our mission is to make Understanding Generative AI for Business Leaders accessible to everyone. Everything we do stems from that mission. And, the only way for us to accomplish that mission is by reaching...well...everyone.

This is where you come in. Most people do, in fact, judge a book by its cover (and its reviews). So here's my ask on behalf of a struggling business leader you've never met:

Please help that business leader by leaving this book a review.

Your gift costs no money and less than 60 seconds to make real, but can change a fellow business leaders life forever. Your review could help...

...one more small businesses provide for their community.

...one more entrepreneur support their family.

...one more employee get meaningful work.

..one more client transform their life.

...one more dream come true.

To get that 'feel good' feeling and help this person for real, all you have to do is...and it takes less than 60 seconds...

leave a review.

Simply scan the QR code below to leave your review:

If you feel good about helping a faceless [TARGET READER], you are my kind of person. Welcome to club. You're one of us.

I'm that much more excited to help you [ACHIEVE TARGET OUTCOMES] [FASTER/EASIER/MORE] than you can possibly imagine. You'll love the [TACTICS/LESSONS/STRATEGIES] I'm about to share in the coming chapters.

Thank you from the bottom of my heart. Now, back to our regularly scheduled program-ming.

- Your biggest fan, Synergy AI Editions

PS - Fun fact: If you provide something of value to another person, it makes you more valuable to them. If you'd like goodwill straight from another Business Leader - and you believe this book will help them - send this book their way.

SCAN ME

Made in the USA
Monee, IL
02 December 2024

72015950R00105